THE ART OF
Calligraphy

hinkler

Alphabet 'nib rating'

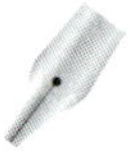

Straightforward letter construction.
Suitable for beginners.

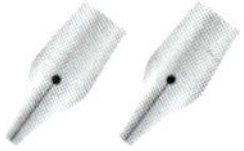

A bit tricky in places.

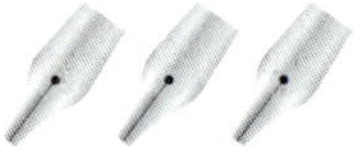

For after you have practised other styles.
This alphabet may need changes for pen angle, pen twists or draining with the corner of the nib.

hinkler

Published by Hinkler Pty Ltd
45–55 Fairchild Street
Heatherton Victoria 3202 Australia
www.hinkler.com

Calligraphy artwork created by and reproduced with the kind permission of Olive Bull (page 33), Nathalie Tousnakhoff (title page and page 45), Colleen Little (title page and page 46), Tricia Smout (page 54), Vincent Geneslay (page 60), Laurant Pflughaupt (page 61), Massimo Polello (title page and page 61), Julie Williams (title page and page 62)

Calligraphy artwork on title page and page 13 created by Gaynor Goffe and reproduced with the kind permission of Barbara Nichol, The Pen Shoppe.
Calligraphy artwork on page 56 created by Ann Hechle and reproduced with the kind permission of Barbara Nichol, The Pen Shoppe.

Photo credit: page 4, © Shutterstock.com; page 9, © Marek Slusarczyk/Shutterstock.com; page 32 and 54, © Mediamix photo/Shutterstock.com; page 44, © OlgaLis/Shutterstock.com

Author: Peter Taylor
Design: Sam Grimmer
Typesetting: MPS Limited

ISBN: 978 1 4889 4360 7

Printed and bound in China

Table of Contents

Introduction to Calligraphy..4

Four Famous Alphabets..9

Creative and Decorative Letters 32

Designing Letters...44

Using Your Calligraphy..54

Introduction to Calligraphy

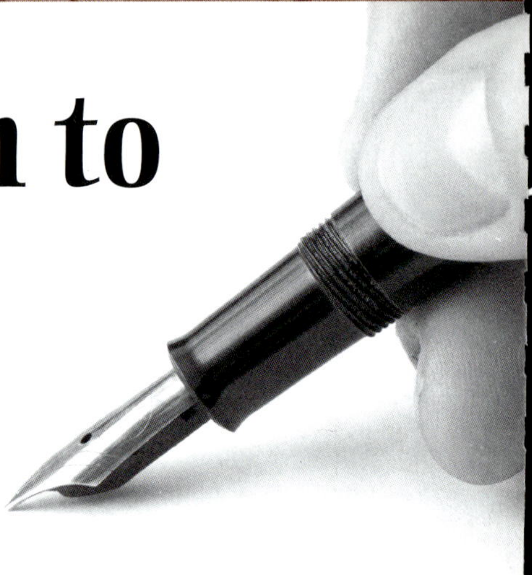

MY DICTIONARY SAYS that calligraphy means 'beautiful handwriting', but these days, calligraphy is a lot more than that because letters can also be engraved into glass, carved into stone and wood, modelled in clay and created as pop-up sculptures. A single letter can also be decorated to produce a bookmark gift featuring the initial letter of someone's name, or just a work of art.

Back in the early days of handwritten books, all lines of writing were straight and evenly spaced. Over the last few years, instead of using letters and words traditionally, calligraphers have experimented with treating them like brush strokes in a picture; as little parts of an overall design. Lines of writing may now be uneven, curved or spiralled, or the letters jumbled to create particular special effects. Though most calligraphy is done with a square-ended, chisel-shaped pen nib that produces thick and thin letter strokes, from time to time today's calligraphers may choose to use any item they can think of that will produce a visible mark.

The aim of this book is to help you enjoy 'the artistic design and use of hand-created letters', which is my definition of calligraphy.

Enjoyment of calligraphy doesn't only come from producing a beautiful end result. It also comes from expressing your feelings in the flow, rhythms and patterns of letter shapes, similar to the way dancers express themselves in a performance. In order to communicate their personal response to the text, a calligrapher will choose a suitable letter style, ink or paint colour and, perhaps, a small range of flourishes that will help demonstrate a particular mood or purpose.

When you watch the best dancers, you admire their smooth body movements in time with the music. You notice if a dancer stumbles or does something that doesn't quite fit in with the rest of the steps. If a dancer enters a competition, the judges will be looking for certain steps or sequences that must be completed.

It's very similar with calligraphy. People may notice when letters are not spaced evenly, one or two are a bit crooked and not all seem to have the right family shape. Just as you and your friends can enjoy dancing wildly at a party, sometimes, in calligraphy it doesn't matter if you make an error or two if the overall look of the finished piece is good, or if you had a lot of fun creating it. On other occasions, however, you do need to be a bit more careful, and if someone tells you that they want a poem written in Italic style, they will expect the letters to have particular features.

AUTHOR'S NOTE

I'll let you in on a secret: my calligraphy is neat, but my handwriting is quite messy and I wish it was better. Calligraphy, for me, is carefully producing each letter as a drawing and placing it in the right spot. It's a totally separate skill from everyday handwriting, though some people do choose to base their handwriting on a calligraphy style.

Learning calligraphy

This book will show you how to enjoy calligraphy – to write and draw letters and create finished work. It will also help you understand what to aim for when you want to write in particular styles and do precise work. It's a feature of being human that our hands don't always follow the instructions given by our brains. Even experts usually manage to find something in their finished piece of calligraphy that they wish they could change. Most artists feel the same about their paintings. But we have to aim for perfection. There is more chance of producing impressive writing and letter shapes if we understand the principles of their construction and how styles fit in to the history of writing. And like learning to play a musical instrument, the more you practise, the better you get and eventually you rarely need to think about the letter shapes and rhythms of different styles. When these come automatically, you can then concentrate on good spacing and working artistically . . . and you make fewer spelling mistakes (they're easily made when you're thinking of several things at the same time).

Developing technique

You, too, will add your own character to your writing, and everyone has their own ideas on beauty of arrangement.

To enable you to express yourself using calligraphy, you will probably want to collect a 'tool box' of techniques and writing styles that you can select from and which you enjoy using. My job is to help you understand the principles or rules of good letter construction in styles you will use as a basis for your own. With practice, you'll become confident as a craftsperson, knowing what you are doing and why. People will recognise this confidence in your artwork – it's the hallmark of the finest calligraphy.

What you need to get started

You don't need that much to get started. In fact, you probably already have all that you need.

As you'll soon discover, it's a good idea to first draw letters with a single line – with a pencil, ball-point pen, fine technical pen or fibre-tip pen. Any smooth paper they'll easily write on will be just fine. If you're keen to recycle and save the planet, you can write on the backs of used envelopes, around the borders of magazines or on advertising junk mail, but if you're buying paper for practice, the cheapest is probably photocopier or laser printer paper.

I imagine that you'll use normal fountain-pen ink for some time. Black or dark blue (or any dark colour) are best because they show up well on paper. The ink will fade rapidly, but is fine for practice – you won't produce a masterpiece for a while.

Calligraphy felt pens with chisel-shaped tips rapidly wear out – sometimes after less than a page of practice. If you own one, I'd keep it for an occasional letter or two when you have sharpened your skills.

Many people will already own a calligraphy fountain pen or set of pens. They all work well. I use one for much of the calligraphy work that people pay me to do. If you are going to buy this kind of pen, it's probably worth going to a specialist pen store to purchase one that you can refill from a bottle of ink, rather than having to keep using cartridges. Cartridge ink will eventually fade, but you can buy fade-proof ink in bottles.

If you are buying a pen with only one **nib**, choose a nib that's about 2 mm (1/16 in) or more wide to learn with – the wider the better. Sets of pens usually come with a nib of this size, plus one smaller and one bigger one.

If you get hooked on calligraphy, you will probably buy a complete pen for each nib size that you regularly use.

Also in my recommended kit of things to start with are more items you'll probably already have:

- Ruler (preferably clear plastic)
- 2 HB pencils
- Sticky tape
- Scissors
- The side of a corrugated-cardboard box

And that's all you'll need at first.

Preparing to write

Position and posture

The best place to write is generally by a window on the shaded side of the house. If you're right-handed, have the light coming from the left and vice versa. At night, try to sit so that a light provides illumination from a similar direction. An adjustable lamp should ensure you always have the light in the right place, but be careful as some may get too hot.

You have to be comfortable to write well, sitting with a straight back, square on to the board you'll use and the table supporting it, and with both feet on the floor.

Writing board and surface

Some people buy fancy hinged constructions for their writing board or prop it up on paper-covered bricks, but I'm sure most calligraphers are like me and have the bottom edge in their lap and by moving closer or further away from the table, can alter the board's slope. I also have a favourite chair with arms that I often use to support my board.

The aim is for your forearm to rest completely on the board with your writing hand at least a third of the way down from the top. This keeps you steady and gives you better hand and finger control.

Changing the slope of the board lets you control the speed at which the ink or paint flows from the pen – a shallow board angle makes you hold the pen more upright, and the ink flows quicker. A shallow sloping board also gives you a better view of what you're doing. You get a less distorted perspective.

If you were just to put your paper straight on to the board to write, you'd probably find the surface feels too hard. Calligraphy pens work best, and you get better results, if the writing paper has a little bit of give or springiness under it, so it's a good idea to create a pad where you will write. Some calligraphers cover nearly their whole board in 10 or more sheets of flat newspaper and tape a large sheet of cartridge paper over the top for cleanliness.

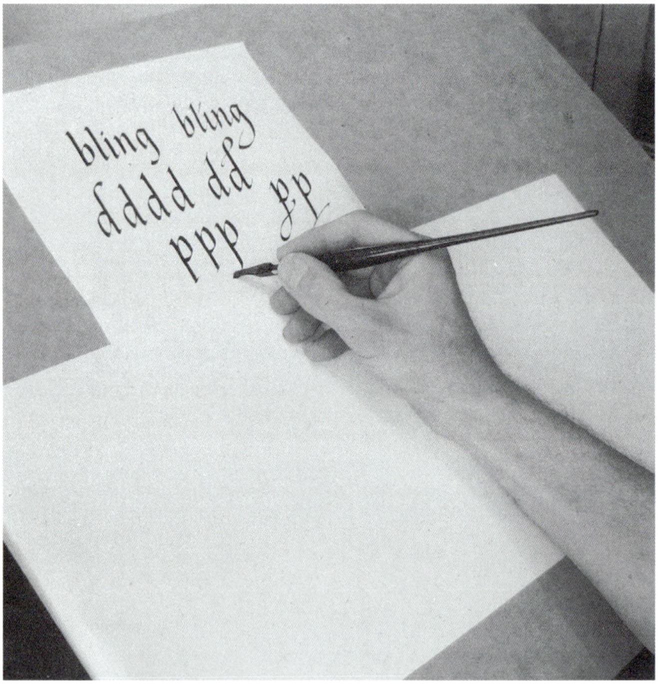

The steep slope of the board means that the pen is held nearly horizontally and the speed of paint or ink flow is reduced.

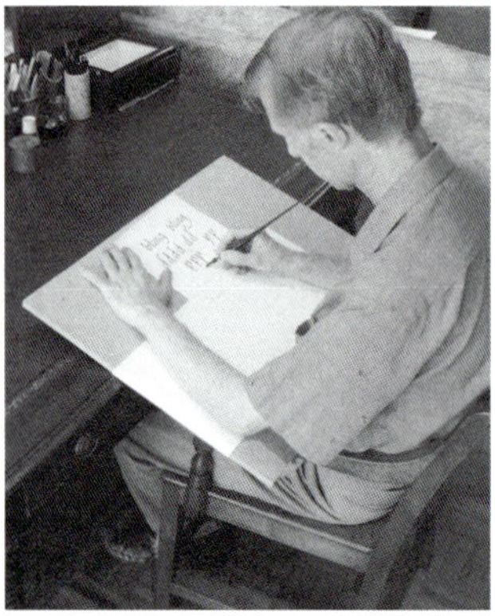

The writing board is supported by the arm of a chair.

I was taught to fold a sheet of newspaper to make a pad about 8 cm (3 in) square. Holding a pencil or pen, I let my writing hand rest where it feels most natural and comfortable, and then I tape my small pad to the board so that the writing implement tip is about in the middle. I also tape a small piece of clean white paper, only just larger than the newspaper, over the top. By only writing in this area, I find that I keep letters more consistently on the same slope. My non-writing hand is used to move the writing paper to a new position after every few letters or when I reach the edge of the pad.

One of the things that can cause ink to bleed into the paper is if oil and sweat from your hand gets rubbed into the surface. You should always write with your hand resting on some scrap paper. This is called a guard sheet and it should be fixed to one side of your board so that your writing paper will slot behind it and you'll comfortably write just above its edge.

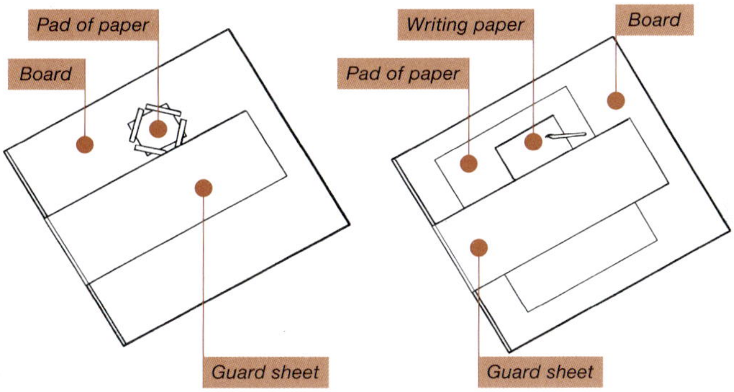

Ruling lines on paper

When copying a writing style, you'll want to know how tall the letters should be. Books on calligraphy often tell you the height of the small letter 'x' of a particular style, expressed in 'nib-widths' – this is known as the 'x-height'. You can decide for yourself what height you want to make the letters compared to your pen size.

Whatever pen you are going to use, you'll need to make a stack of short lines, just touching each other, on a scrap piece of paper and mark the top and bottom, as shown below.

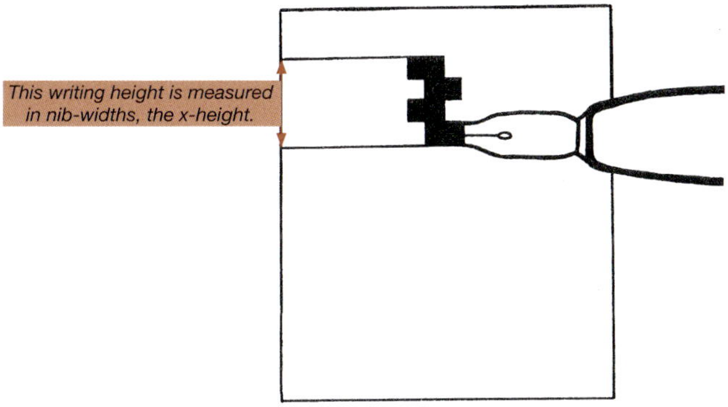

It will largely be a matter of your own personal taste how far apart you want to make the lines of writing – it certainly won't matter for practice.

On the same piece of scrap paper, using a pencil, mark off how far down you want the top of the next line of writing – for example, a 'stack and two-thirds'.

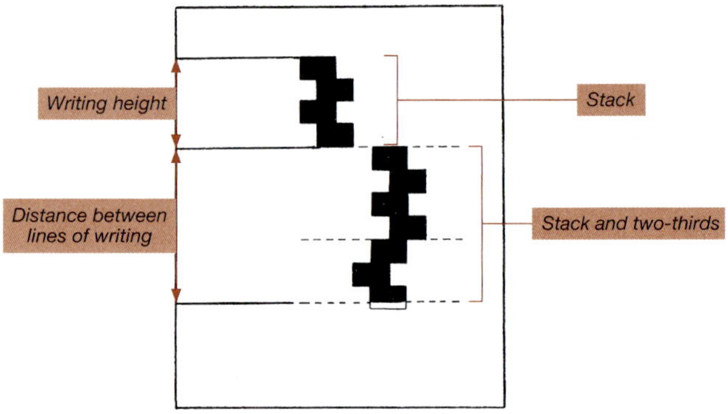

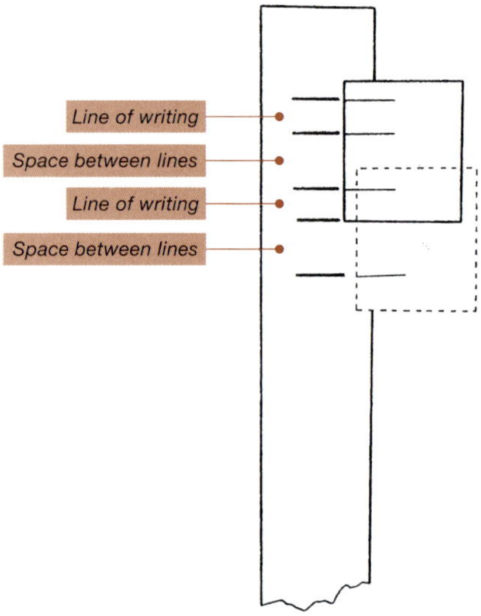

This piece of scrap paper becomes a 'marking out tool'. Next, again from scrap paper, cut a long strip that's at least as long as your writing sheet, and mark on it where you want the top of the first line of writing.

Using this tool, you can then mark off the bottom of the first writing line onto the strip, and the top edge of the next writing line down. Then move the tool to mark off the bottom of the second line and the next space, and so on.

You can then lay the strip on the top of your finished sheet and, using a tee-square, lightly draw your guidelines using a sharp H-grade pencil. The strip can be kept to mark up other sheets at another time.

If you don't have a tee-square, don't worry – just cut the long strip of paper in half after you have marked it out, cutting each line mark in two. All you have to do is tape one half-strip on the left of your writing paper and the other on the right and then 'join the dots' with a pencil and ruler.

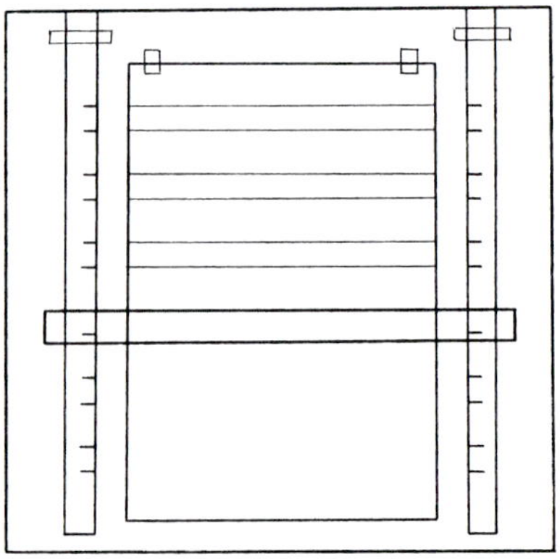

AUTHOR'S NOTE

Before taping things on to good paper, reduce the sticking power of the tape by pressing it on to fabric a few times and it will be less likely to leave a mark.

If you've taped a lumpy, bumpy pad on your board surface, and maybe a guard sheet, it could be easiest to use the back of the board (or another board kept especially for the purpose) for ruling lines. You may choose to attach your paper to the board while ruling, so that it doesn't slip.

Four Famous Alphabets

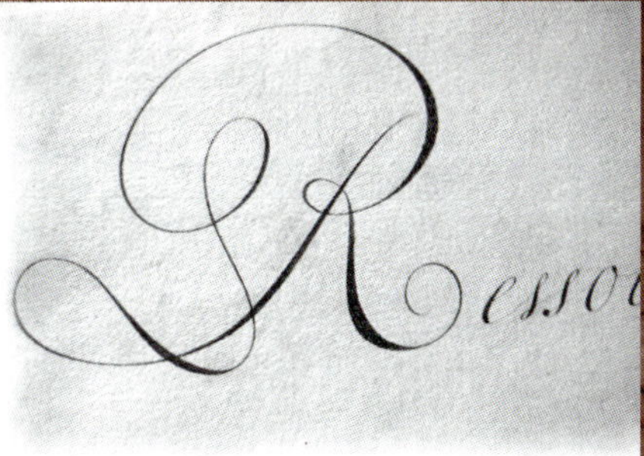

YOU WILL FIND that most instructional calligraphy books will contain the same four alphabet styles that I'm providing here: Foundational Hand, Gothic, Italic and Uncial. Most other alphabets are based on the structures of these ones. There's no need to learn extra fancy tricks or special touches. You'll add your own character to these anyway. If you can write well in the first four of these styles, you'll already be an excellent calligrapher, equipped with all the knowledge you need to do most writing. Though you might choose to make small changes to these styles, add decorations and learn other alphabets later, it is important to begin learning calligraphy by understanding how the letter shapes in these famous styles are created and how they relate to each other. They are built on simple rules, but are not easy to do – no one has yet found instant success with calligraphy.

Like learning to become a good pianist, if you really want to become a good calligrapher, it's best if you can practise every day, even for a short amount of time, rather than practising a lot all at once and then no more for days or weeks. I also recommend that you only attempt to learn one style at a time.

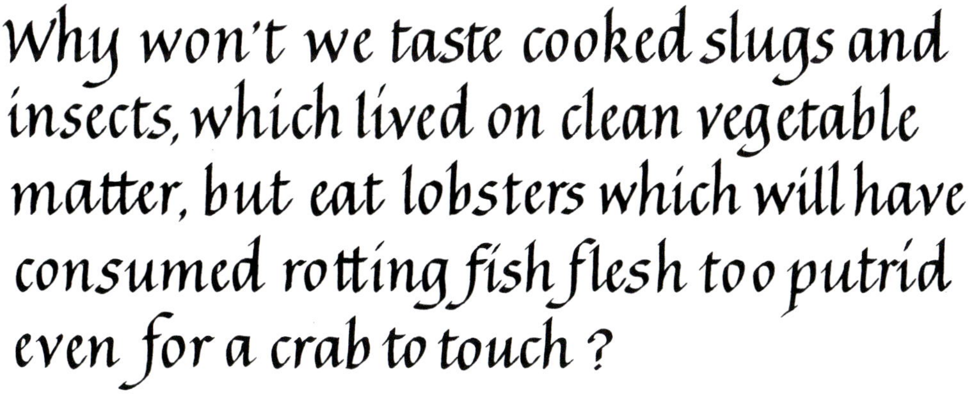

This is a sample of Italic calligraphy, written according to the instructions in this book.

Foundational Hand

Let's start with Foundational Hand, which was first devised by **Edward Johnston** after studying the 10th-century book, ***Ramsey Psalter***, written in a **Carolingian style**.

Why choose to learn Foundational first? It's upright and based on circles, and everyone knows what they look like. Foundational Hand has many features of elegant Roman letters and can also be easily modified to create interesting and useful variations.

As with learning Roman capitals, it's best to first learn the letter shapes and proportions by drawing simple versions with a pencil and fitting them into squares, as shown below. Square-gridded paper is ideal to use to start with, but once you have mastered this, you can then begin to write the letters freehand on plain paper with top and bottom guidelines only.

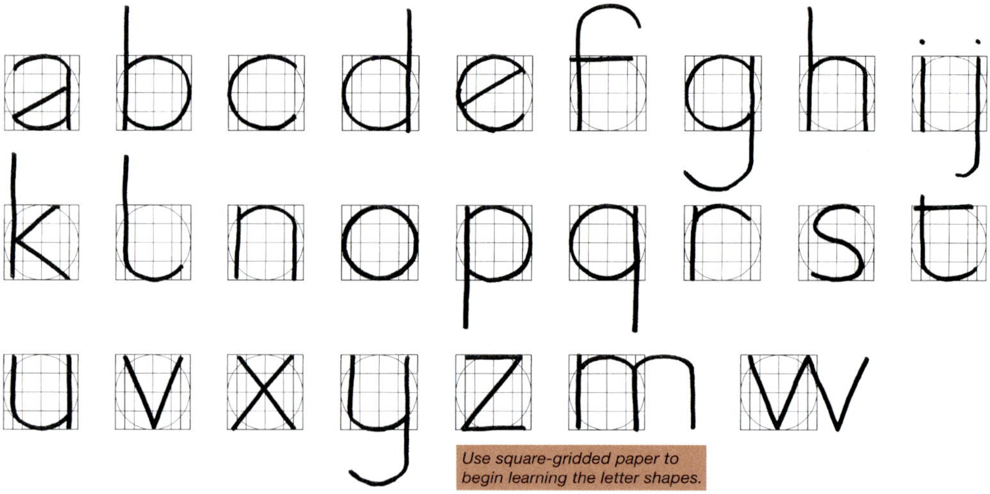

Use square-gridded paper to begin learning the letter shapes.

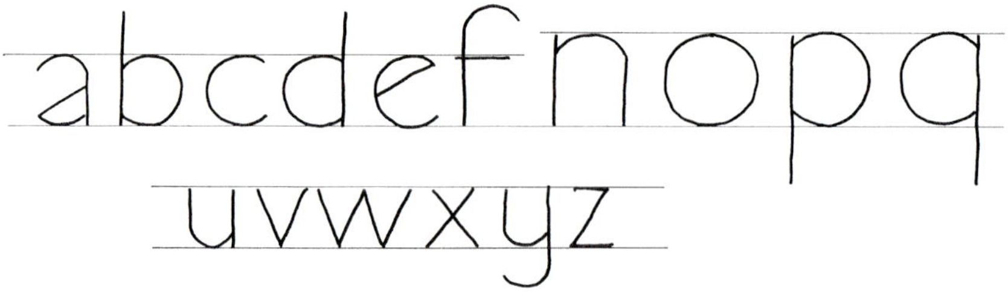

Then you can try spacing out letters to write words. The space between letters should always appear to equal the same area as the white space counter inside the letter 'u', or 'n'.

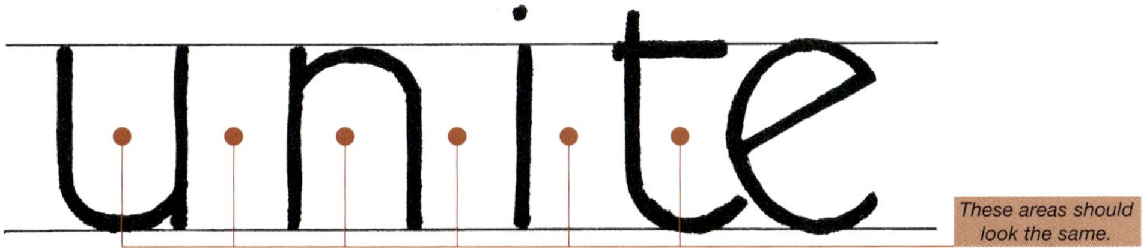

Unfortunately, you can't rely on writing in boxes to space letters – it has to be done by eye. This can get tricky when an 'r' is followed by a 'v' for example. In that case, the top of the 'r' can be shortened, and the left corner of 'v' started fractionally lower than normal and tucked underneath. Similarly, the bar of 't' can be shortened when necessary. I'll show you some more problem-solving tricks later.

The space between words should be about the complete width of the letter 'o', as shown below. If an 'o' touched on to the right-hand end of one word, the following word would be touching the other side of the 'o'.

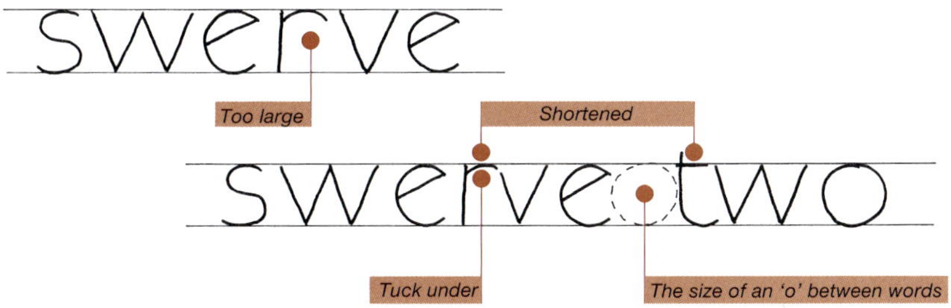

The anatomy of letters

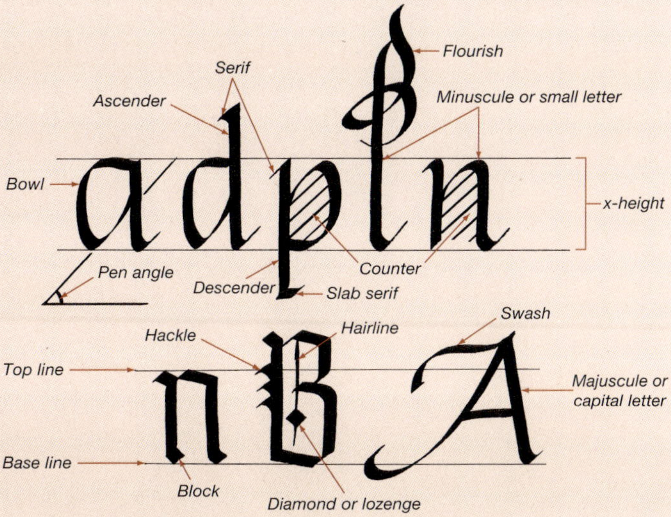

Writing Foundational calligraphy

Now, let's do some thick and thin calligraphy!

Choose a pen with a chisel-edge shaped nib at least 2 mm (1/16 in) wide and load it with ink. Choose the widest nib it feels comfortable to write with.

Draw a 'stack' to discover the height of 4½ **nib-widths**. This will become the **x-height** or body-height of most small letters. Rinse and dry your pen. Next, rule up a sheet of practice paper, using a pencil, with lines 4½ nib-widths apart.

When practising, the space between lines of writing should be at least twice the x-height. When you are doing a finished job with a calligraphy pen in Foundational Hand, twice the x-height or less is a good amount of space.

> **AUTHOR'S NOTE**
> When there are a small number of words per line of writing in any style, you may find the finished piece looks better if the space between lines is reduced.

By drawing with your pen, you will discover how to move and wiggle the nib from side to side to make straight lines that continue at hair thickness (as thin as the nib will make).

For Foundational Hand, you need to hold the pen and the paper so that these thin lines are about 35° to the horizontal. This is the **pen angle**. If you could remove your writing hand from the pen, the pen-handle would drop to land as in the picture below.

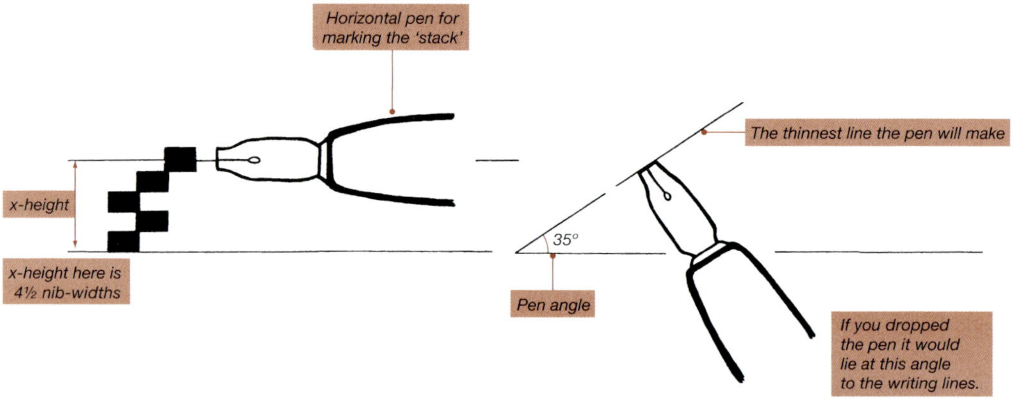

Your paper does not have to be vertical. If it helps you to maintain the correct pen angle, turn the paper a little, especially if you're left-handed.

No matter what part of a letter you draw in this style, your pen always stays at that 35° angle (unless I tell you otherwise!). If you draw a vertical and a horizontal, the horizontal will be the thinner of the two.

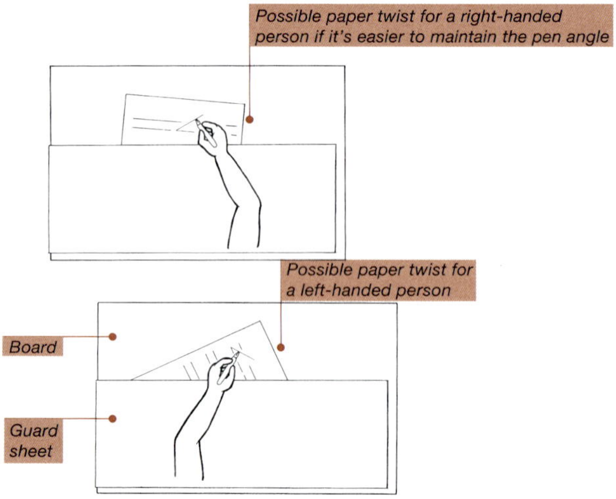

> **AUTHOR'S NOTE**
> Don't forget that your writing hand always stays in the same small area of your board. Your other hand moves the paper after every two or three letters. This helps you to maintain the correct pen angle at all times.

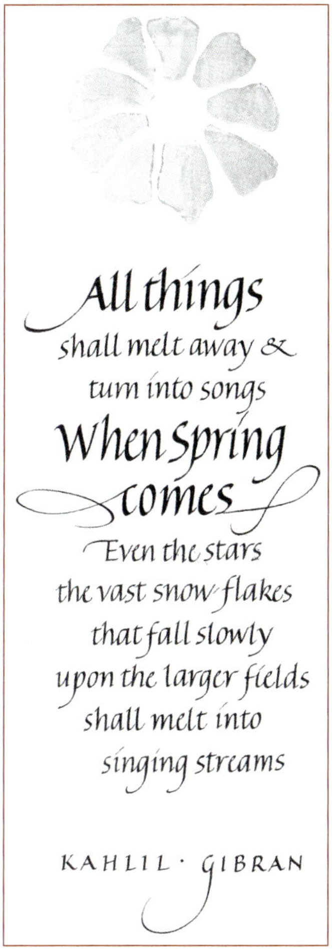

'All Things', by Kahlil Gibran, calligraphy by Gaynor Goffe, a left-handed calligrapher. This artwork is from the collection of Barbara Nichol, The Pen Shoppe, Brisbane
It has been written in Italic. Instructions for italic writing are provided in later pages.

Now, try to draw the same small letter shapes that you drew with a pencil. Remember, you are drawing letters, not writing. You will need to take your pen off the paper and construct many letters in a number of separate strokes.

Although your aim is to write between the guidelines, it's more important to make sure the letter shapes are correct, particularly when practising. Take it above or below the lines if it creates a better shape.

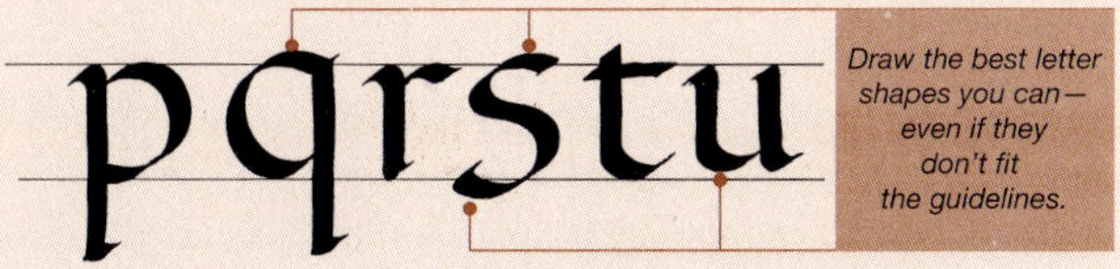

Dip nibs, in particular, do not like being pushed on the paper. They are likely to dig in and the ink could splatter – inevitably on the last word on an important document! Try to get into the habit of always pulling or sliding the pen whether you are using a dip pen, fountain pen or any other implement. It also means you can add attractive 'micro-commas' on the tips of the top element of letters like 'c', 's' and capital 'G', for example.

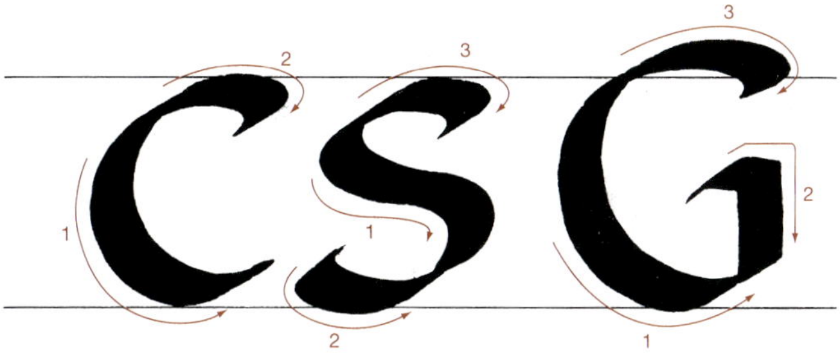

For an 'o', the centre of the pen follows two halves of a circle – left and right, starting close to the top line.

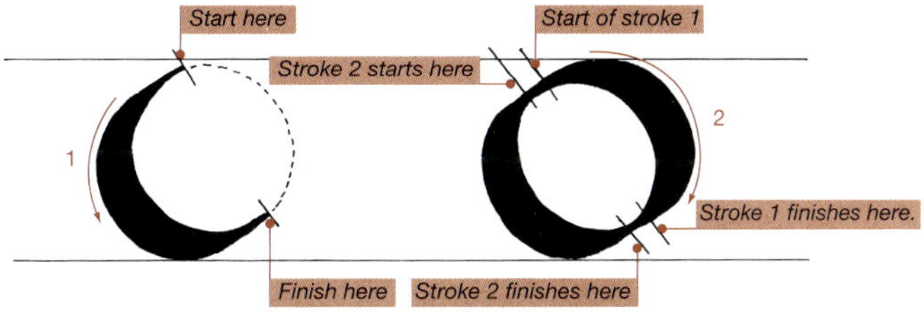

When writing 'n', put the pen nib inside the vertical and start it moving around the arc as you construct the top curve. There should be no thin line showing. The same goes for other letters with rounded tops, and the reverse applies for 'u'.

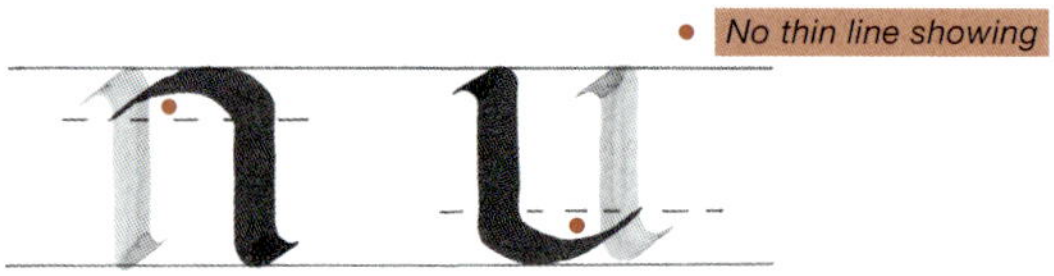

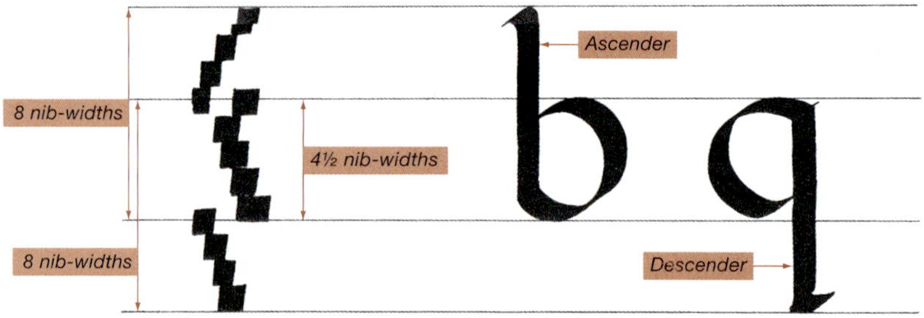

Keep **ascenders** and **descenders** about 8 nib-widths long. Maybe measure the first one, but you don't always need to add a top or bottom guideline for accuracy.

When you can easily draw these shapes, you can add some extra finishing strokes.

Foundational Hand is based on a circular 'o' and so most added **serif** parts also relate to circles. The top serif 'hook' should start curving straight away with no thin line sticking out, while the bottom 'hook' should similarly follow a circle and finish at a point without the thin line showing.

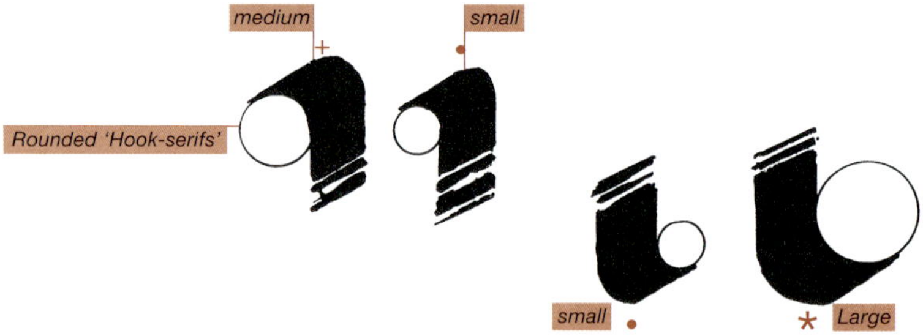

On letters 'u', 'n', 'm' and 'h', the outside hook can be the same size or larger than the ones on the inside limbs.

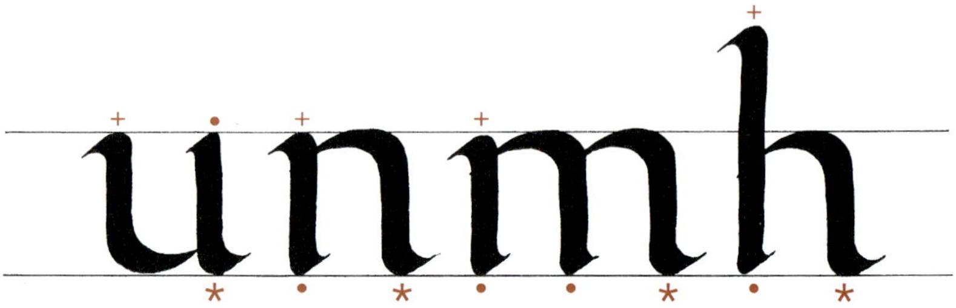

Now, let's try the complete alphabet. Make sure you keep **'slabs'** horizontal.

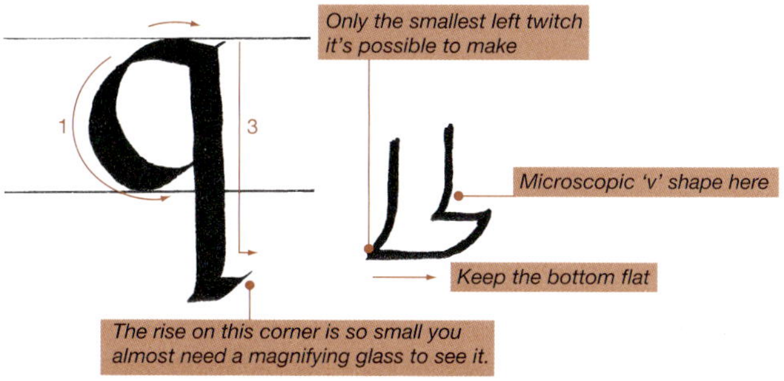

Difficulty Rating

x-height
4½ nib-widths

Pen angle
About 35°

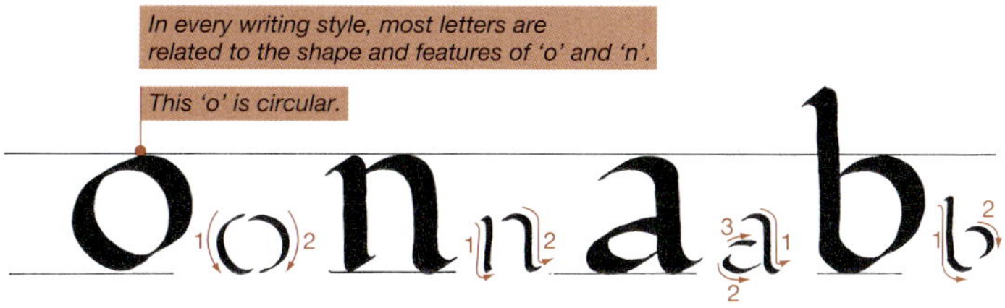

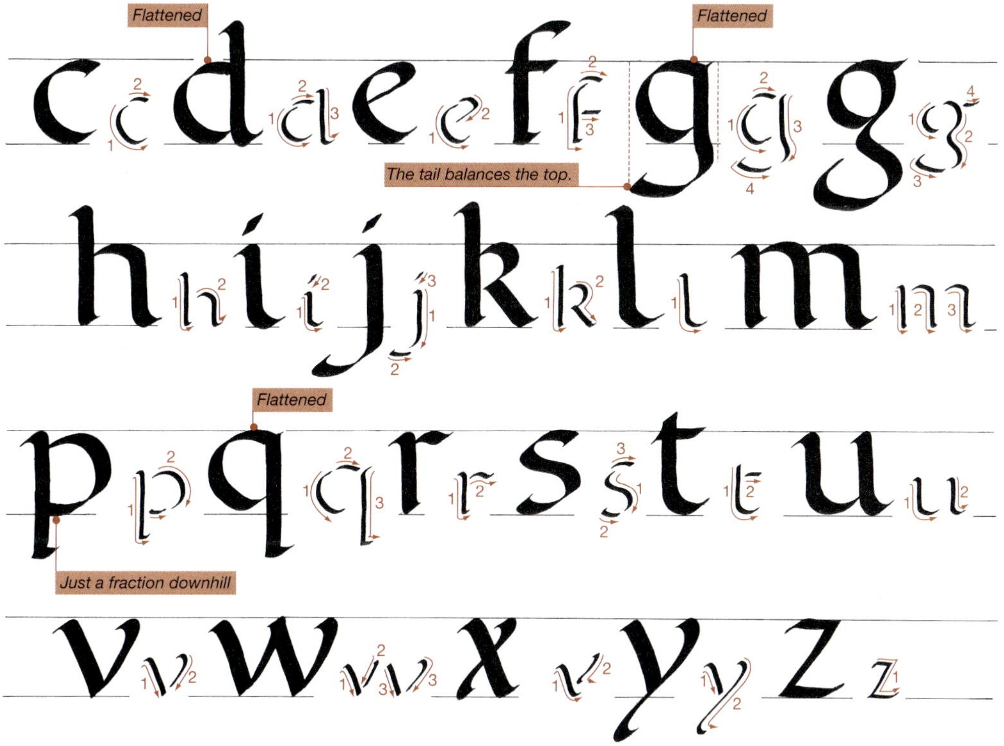

At the time when the *Ramsey Psalter* model was written, all numbers were written in Roman numerals, so there are no old versions like our modern numerals to copy from. Because the alphabet is rounded, just keep the numerals wide, too. You can draw them all the same size, or 'up and down'.

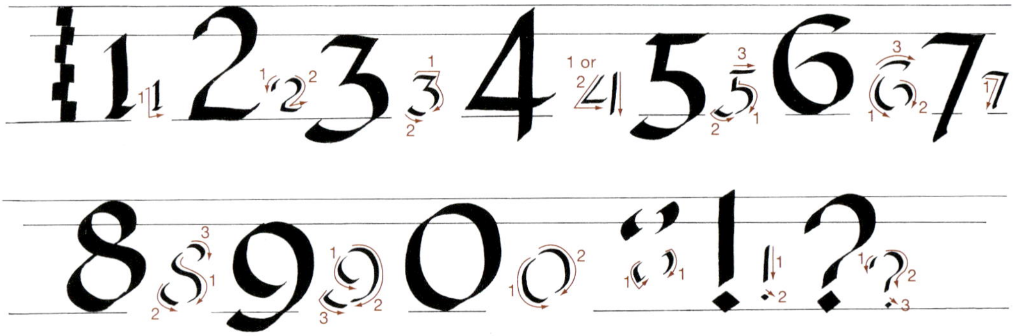

This would have looked better all one size.

This looks attractive and interesting written on two levels.

Even expert calligraphers can struggle with drawing elegant capitals to match Foundational small letters. It's best to make them simple and about 6 nib-widths high.

Keep in mind the classic proportions of the boxed Roman letters, remembering which fit in half a square and three quarters of a square, which bars sit on top of the centre line, under it, and so on.

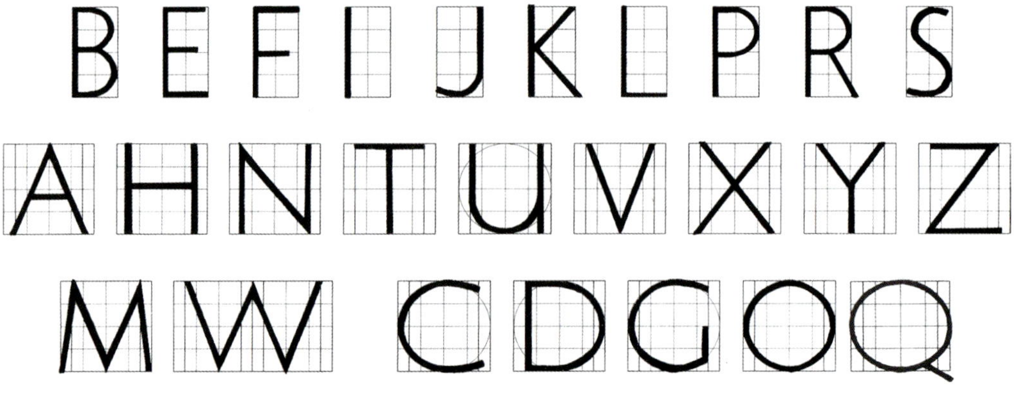

Most serifs will be horizontal slabs or half-slabs.

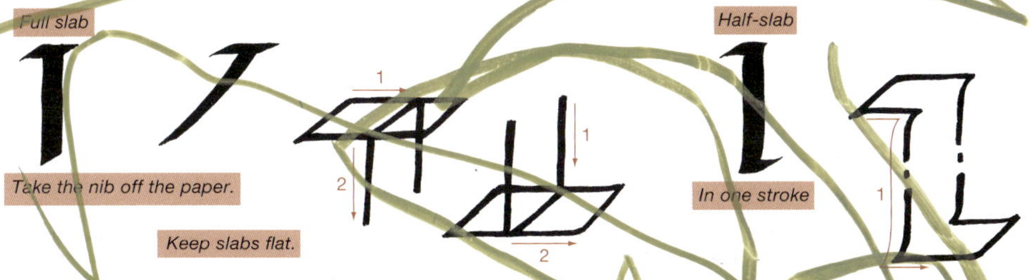

Below is the complete alphabet. This alphabet is straightforward, but not easy. Take your time!

Difficulty Rating

Letter Height
About 6 nib-widths

Pen angle
About 35°

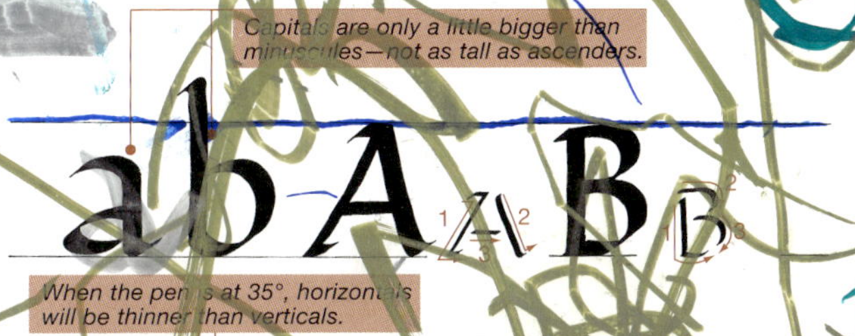

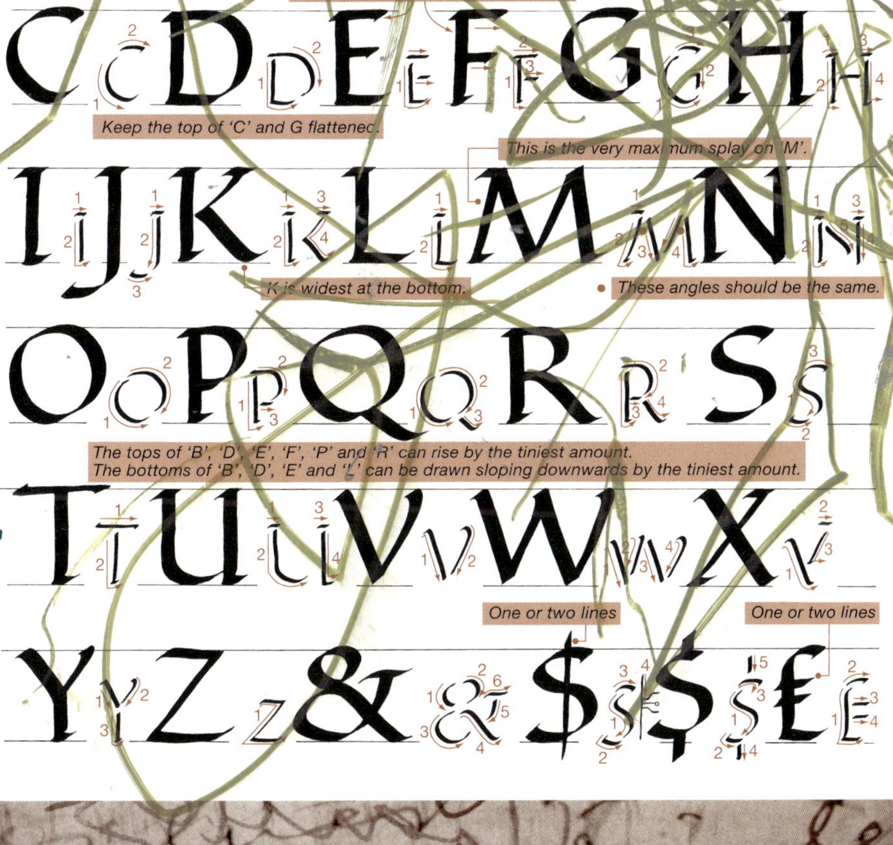

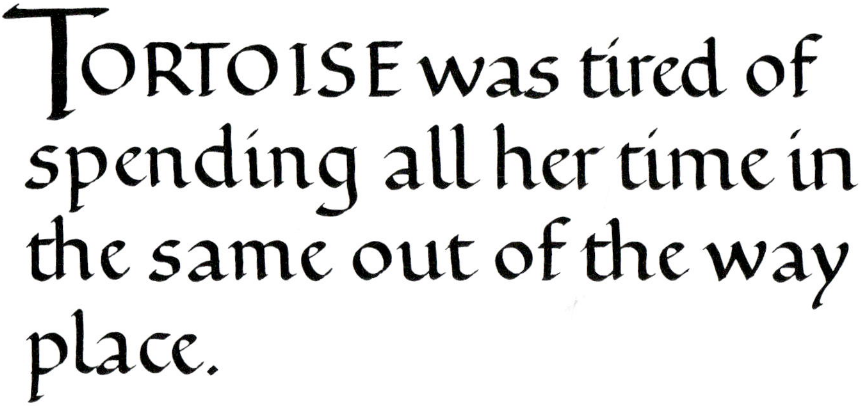

An example of writing in Foundational Hand

Gothic

Gothic or **Black-letter calligraphy** is sometimes thought of as Old English, but Old English is really the name of a typeface, and contains capitals that are hard to copy with a pen.

Gothic script is a natural progression from Foundational Hand. This is because the more you **compress** Foundational Hand, the closer the letters begin to resemble the letters from Gothic script. After as much compression as possible, only slight tweaking of the letters, such as making the corners angular, is needed to transform them into true Gothic script. To explore this, first try squeezing normal Foundational Hand letters from side to side. Make them a little taller – about 5 nib-widths high, like those of the alphabet shown on the right, which still have rounded tops, but also vertical sides.

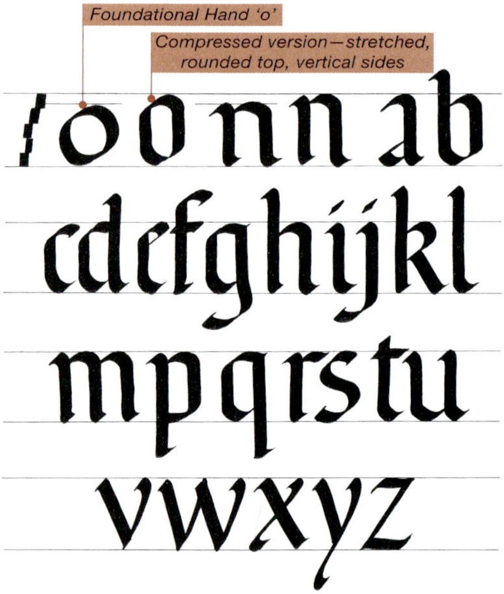

Writing Gothic calligraphy

Construct your letter strokes in the same way as you did for Foundational and Compressed Foundational styles, but make all lines straight and all corners angular.

There are dozens of variations of Gothic script. This simple version is 'Gothic Textura'.

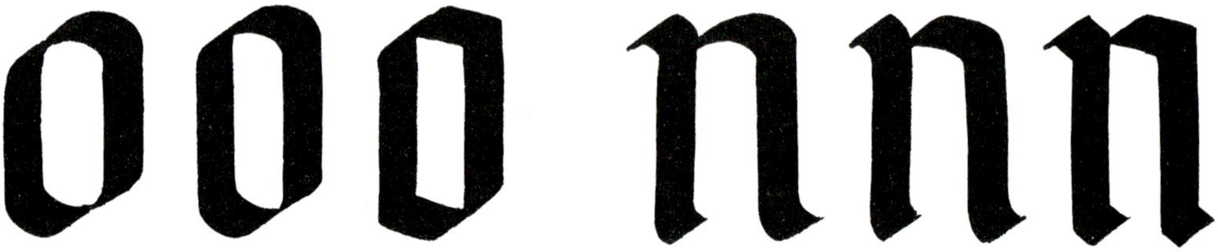

The important thing is that the corners of the blocks should be all on the same level, but not at the same angle.

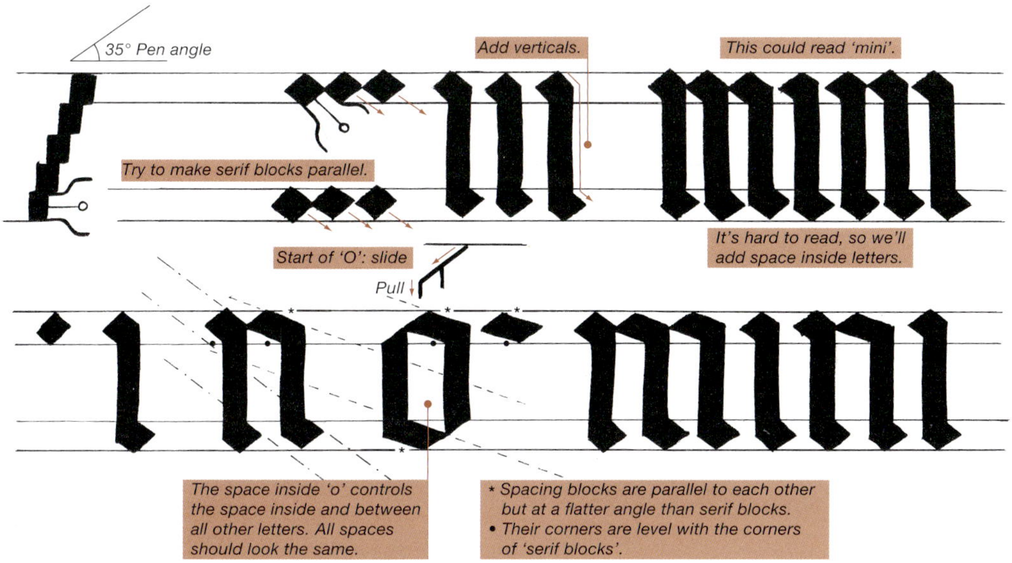

Flattening the joining blocks by just a little should create a white space between strokes that is just a fraction wider than the width of each of the vertical elements.

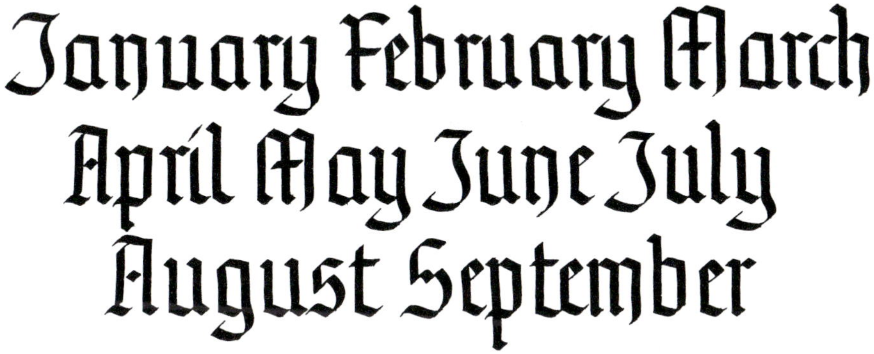

As for all calligraphy, a special effort has been made to make these Gothic letters look well spaced. If you look carefully, you'll find that in some places where you would expect to find blocks at the top of letters, they have been omitted so that the letters were not forced apart, creating gaps that look too large.

Here's the complete alphabet.

Difficulty Rating

x-height
5 nib-widths

Pen angle
About 35°

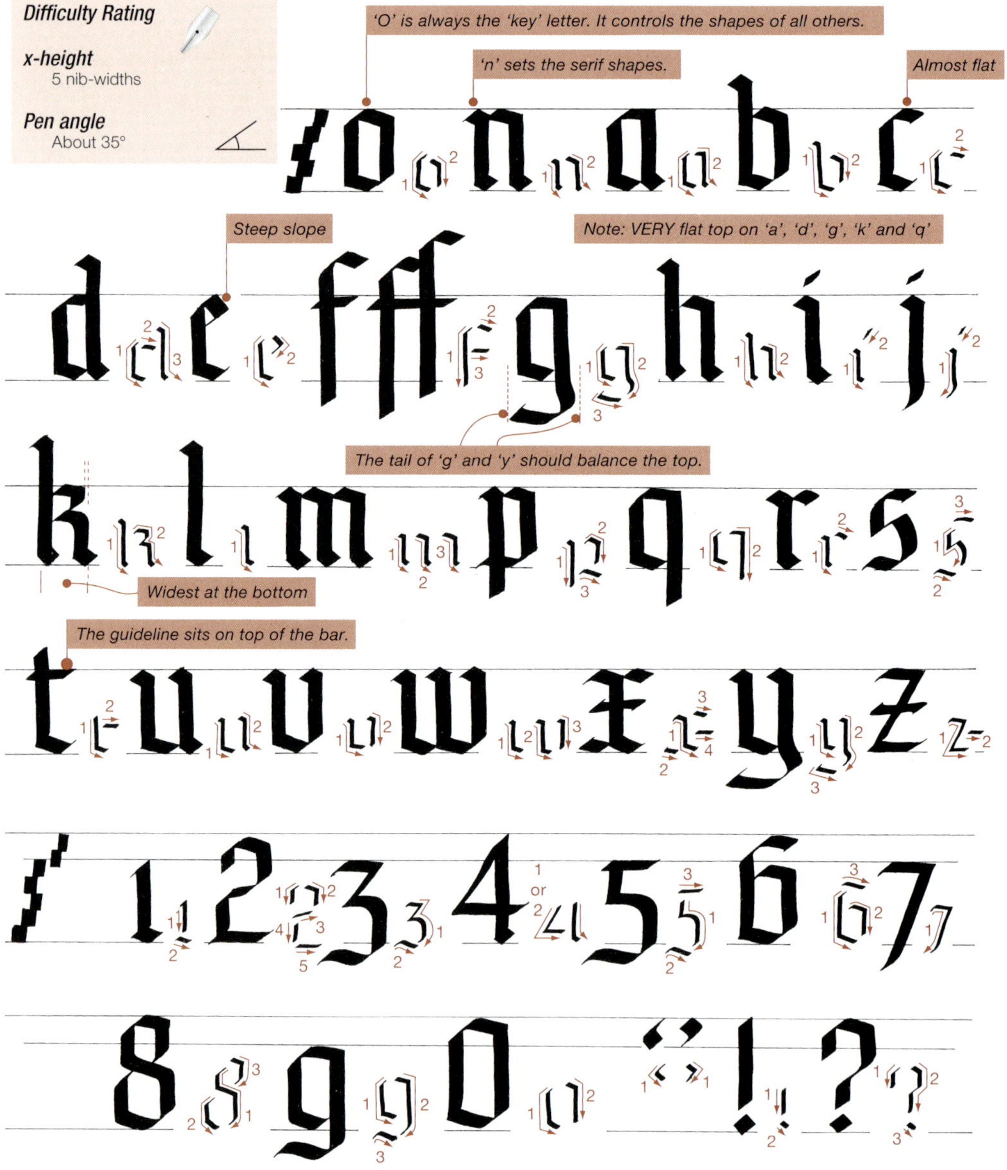

The occasional curve or two can help legibility.

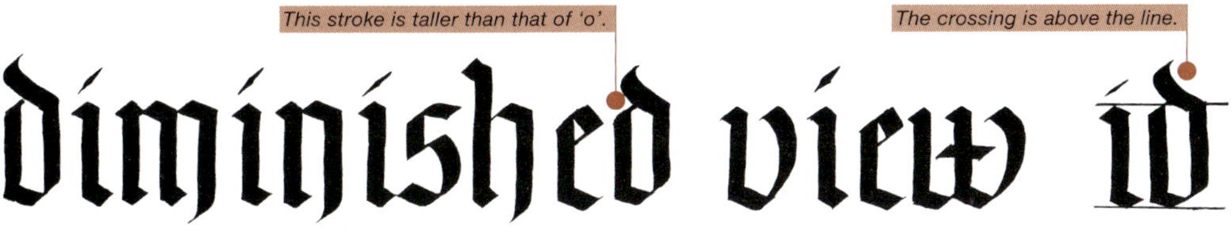

You'll find that every book on calligraphy suggests different shapes for capitals. Originally, most were painted and looked nothing like the ones we use today.

Difficulty Rating

Letter Height
About 6½ nib-widths

Pen angle
About 35°

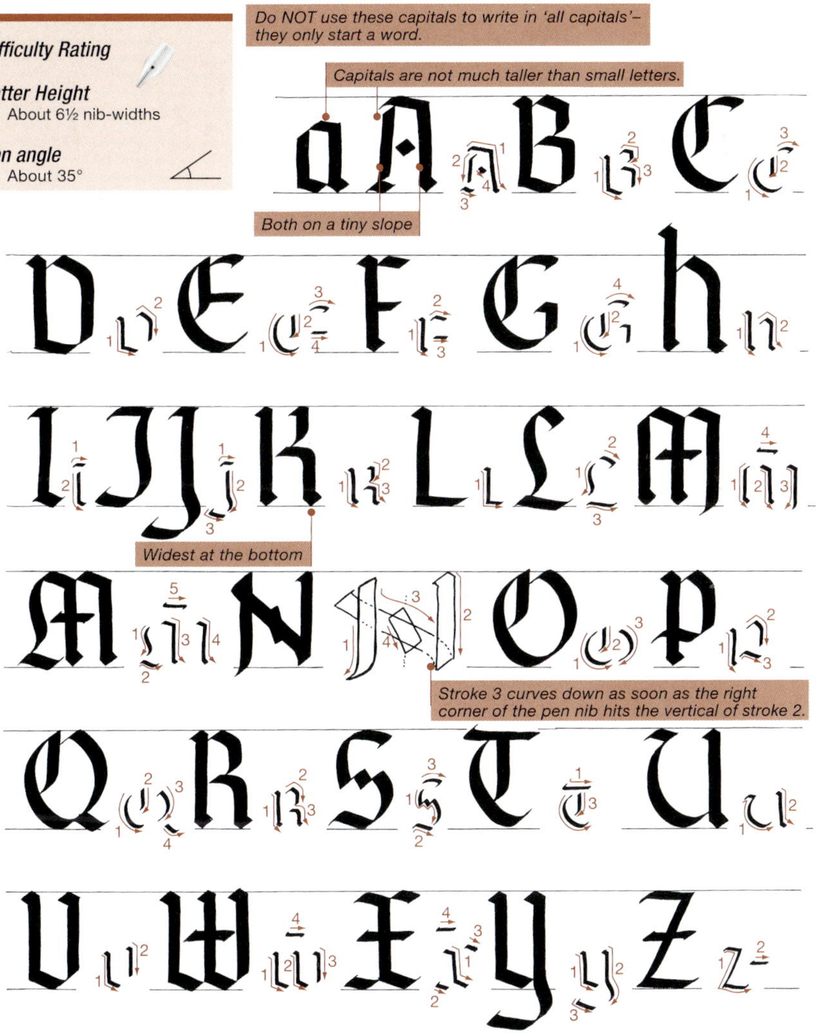

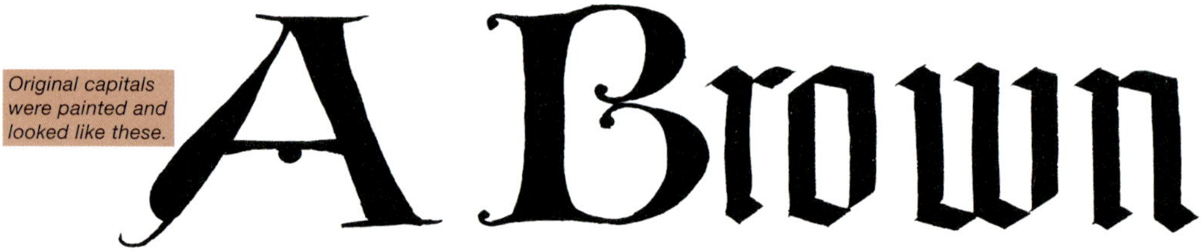

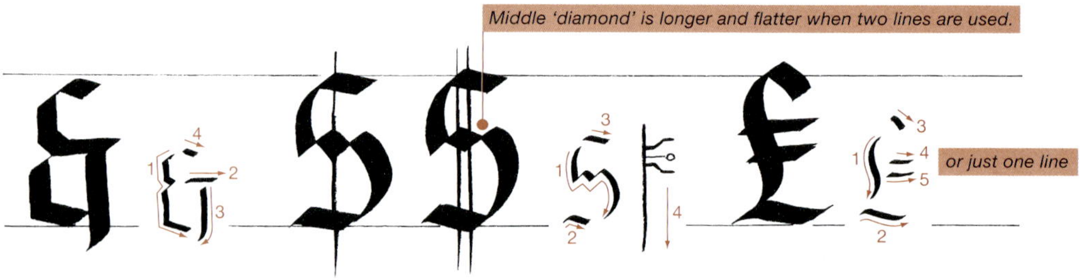

Gothic is also called Black-letter because it produces dense stripes, or blocks of writing. You can experiment with closing the space between lines of writing. When the space is very small, the text will be easiest to read if there are only a few words to each line.

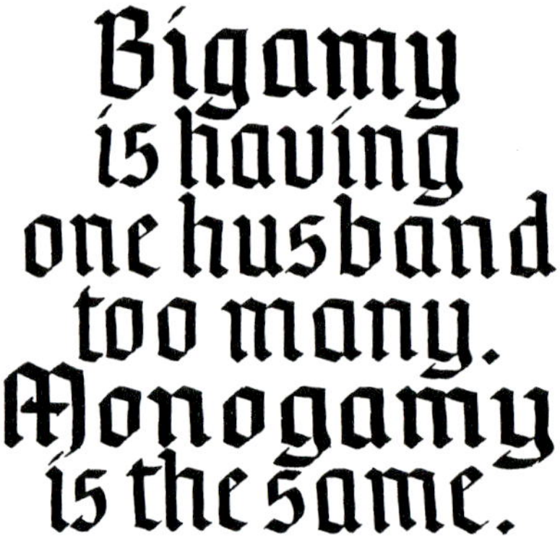

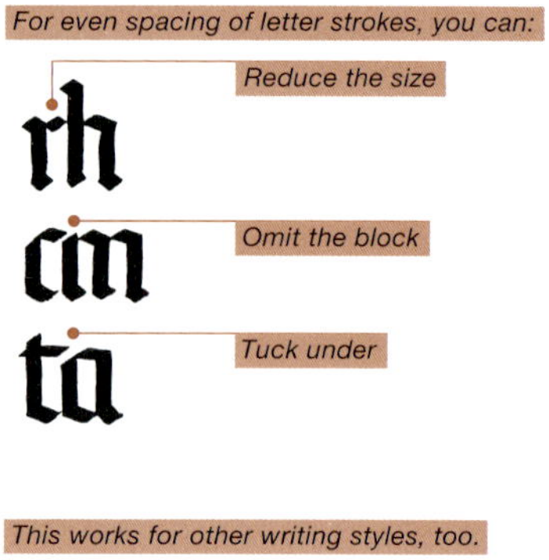

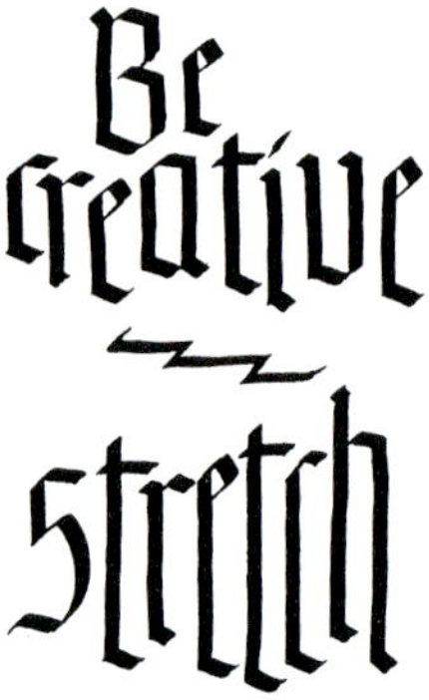

An example of writing in Gothic.

Italic

Over the centuries, Italic script has changed a lot and today calligraphers are still finding new ways to modify letters but retain the underlying principles of construction. Italic dates back to Niccolo Niccoli's bouncy joined handwriting of 1416. Later scribes cut off some of the joining strokes and added extra precision in the drawing of each letter for impressive documents, including copies of the Pope's instructions to be sent to all branches of the Roman Catholic Church in the late 1400s and early 1500s. When wealthy people saw the style, they paid for books to be written out with even greater care and no joins at all between letters. This became known as Formal Italic.

This is a sample of formal Italic

In the mid- to late 1500s, printing was taking over from writing, so scribes such as Arrighi, Cataneo and Tagliente earned money from teaching people how to write. They created rules for proper letter construction and had **copybooks** printed, but it wasn't long before the skills of the original scribes were lost.

Italic handwriting again became increasingly popular during the 20th century, particularly after 1932, when **Alfred Fairbank** designed modernised letters (based on Arrighi's) for student use.

Early Italic writing was incredibly small and it was easy for a worn quill pen to be pushed around the writing surface, but you can't easily push modern metal dip nibs.

Italic calligraphy using large-sized letters has only been popular since the mid-1900s. It shares many features with Italic handwriting, but is not just a larger version. As with Foundational and Gothic styles, many of the calligraphic Italic letters are constructed in several separate strokes.

The two main characteristics of Italic are that the letter 'o' is compressed – it's elliptical – and the arch shape on 'n' branches out from the vertical.

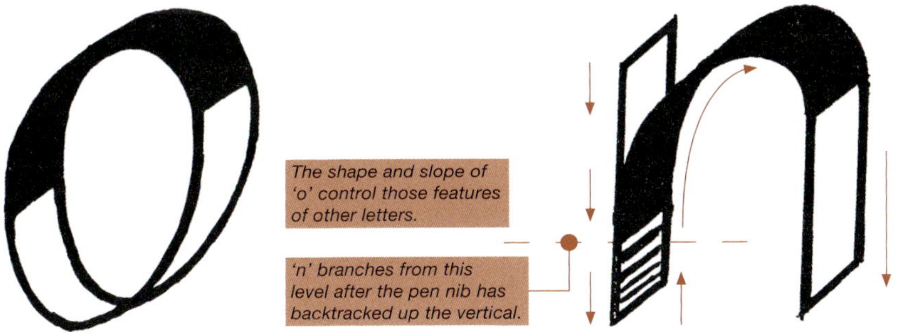

The Italic writing style is often called the script of 'branching arches'. Like all other alphabets, it is controlled by the shape of the letter 'O'. Because it is narrow, so are all the other letters. When written with 'bounce', it is usually also slightly sloped, because slope comes naturally as speed is increased. To start with, and also for important documents like certificate designs, it's best to keep letters nearly upright. The branch feature comes when drawing an 'n' and related letters. Having reached the bottom of the vertical, the writing implement stays on the paper, backtracks a tiny distance back up the vertical and then branches out and heads in a smooth arc towards the top right hand corner of the letter, where a sharp but rounded turn is made before descending parallel to the first stroke.

Try the alphabet first as **skeleton letters** as shown below. The top right-hand corner of 'u' and related letters is the reverse of the bottom left-hand corner of 'n' – the sloping line of 'u' is pushed vertically as it finishes, and this tip is covered over as the right-hand side descends. Then write the letters with tiny entry and exit strokes. Pointed 'tick' entries can be added to the tops of 'i', 'l', 'v', 'u', 'w', 'y', 'j', 'h', 'b', 'p' and 'k'. The exit strokes are rounded and, if extended, would be lines drawn at about 45°. The reverse is used for the rounded entry strokes to 'n', 'm', 'r' and 'x'.

Capitals are best kept simple and with classic proportions, though perhaps with all of them squashed a little from side to side, too. Note how a capital 'A' will fit into the wedge shapes created on branching Italic letters. Also note the relationship between 'b' and 'g'.

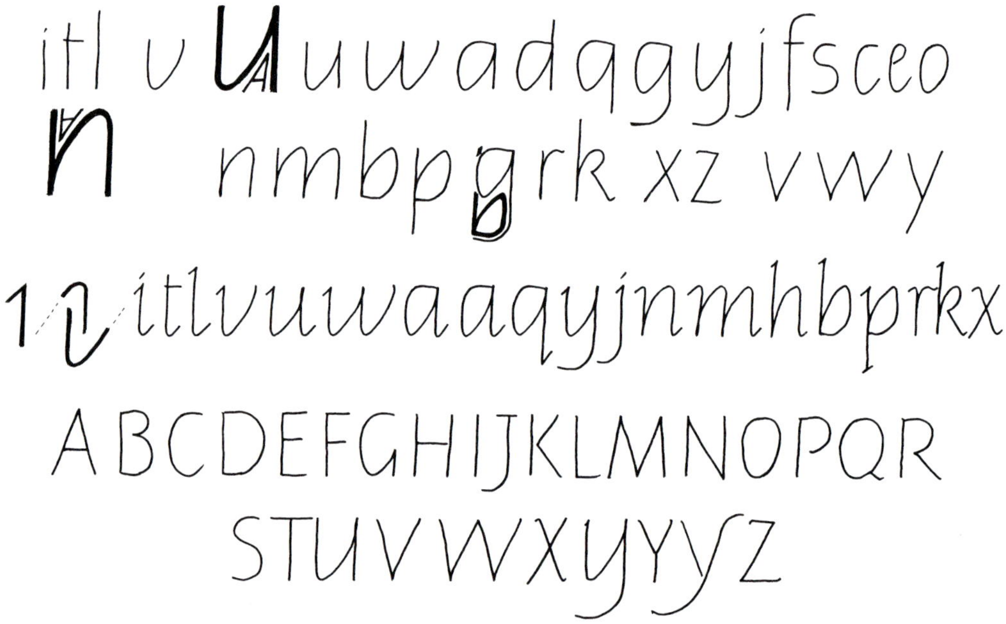

When writing thick and thin calligraphy for any given lettering style, 99% of the time, the pen should be held at a constant angle to the writing line – for an upright Italic this is about 45° (it can be good to increase the pen angle when writing the verticals on a letter 'N', for example). Remember, it's often easiest to maintain this 45° angle if you move the paper every few letters.

Writing Italic calligraphy

The usual x-height of Italic small letters (minuscules) is five times the width of the nib (5 pen-widths or nib-widths). This alphabet is built in families of letters.

Difficulty Rating

x-height
5 nib-widths

Pen angle
About 45°

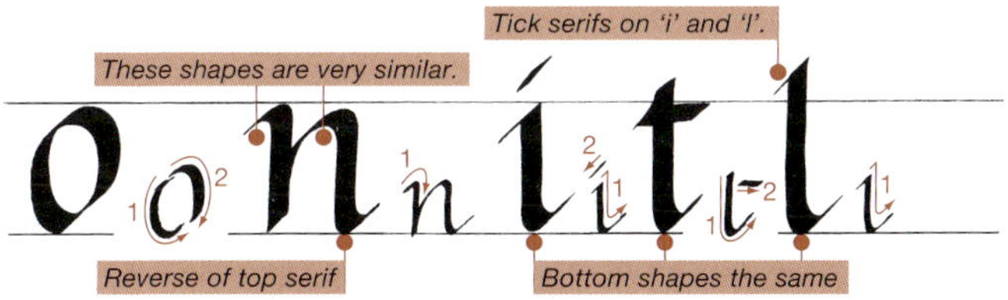

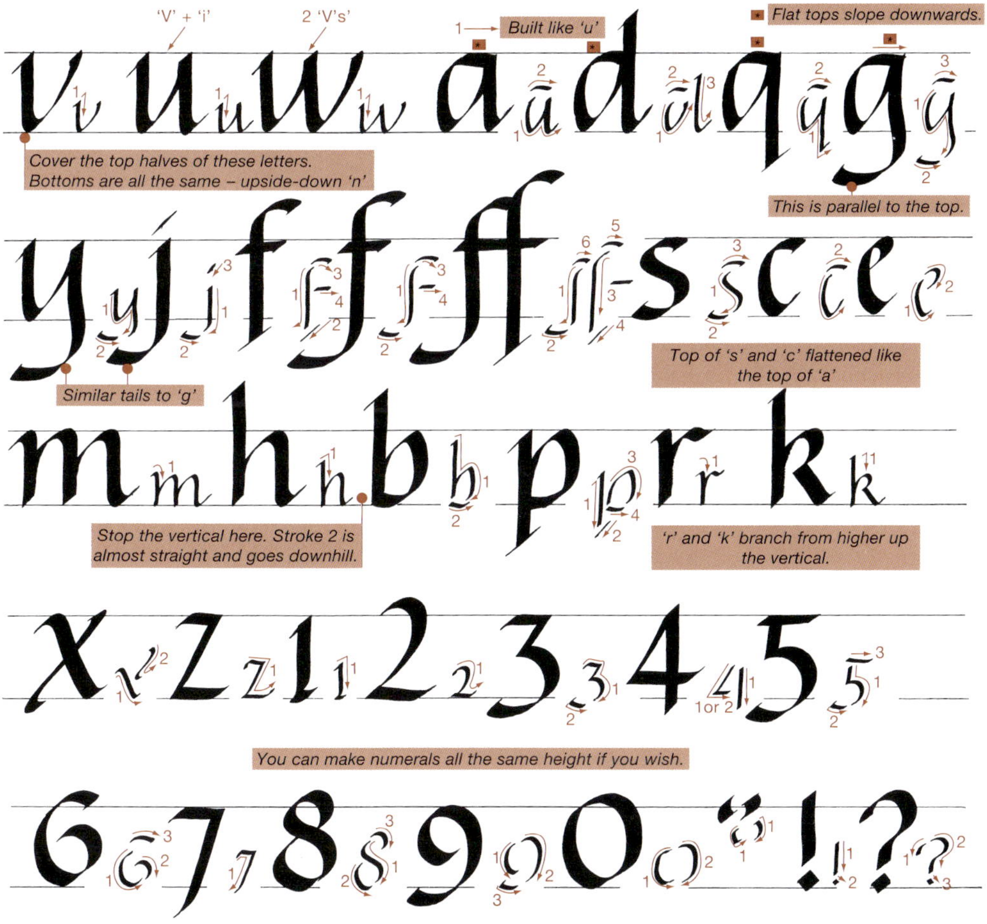

Some alternative letters are shown below.

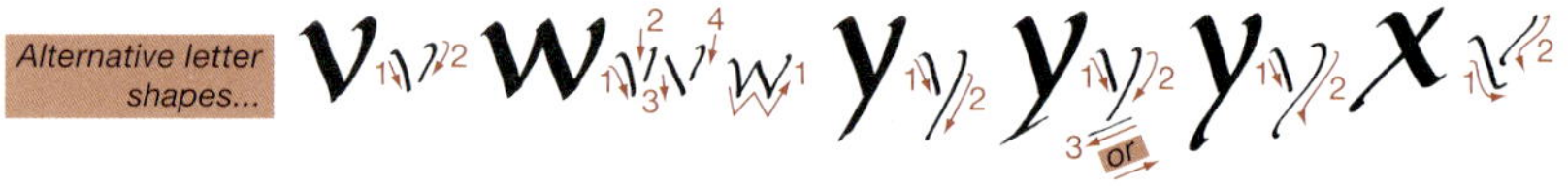

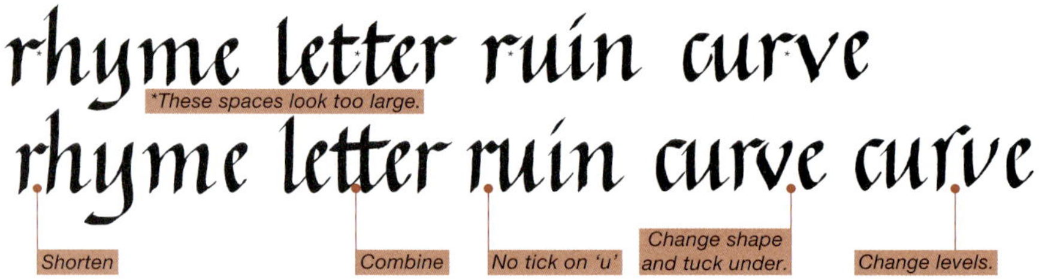

Italic capitals are 6½ nib-widths high. They can be less sloped and compressed than the small letters. Most capitals look best when drawn only a small amount taller than minuscules.

Difficulty Rating

Letter Height
About 6½ nib-widths

Pen angle
About 45°

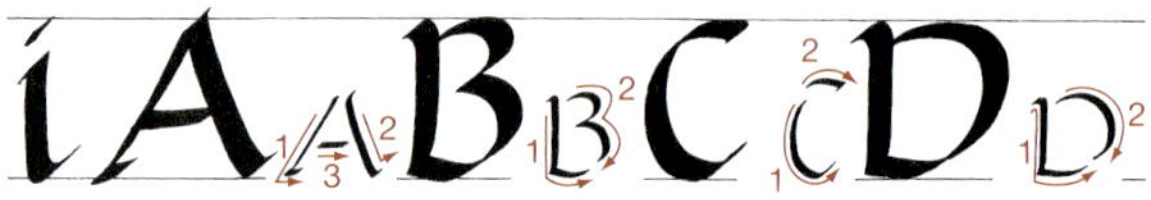

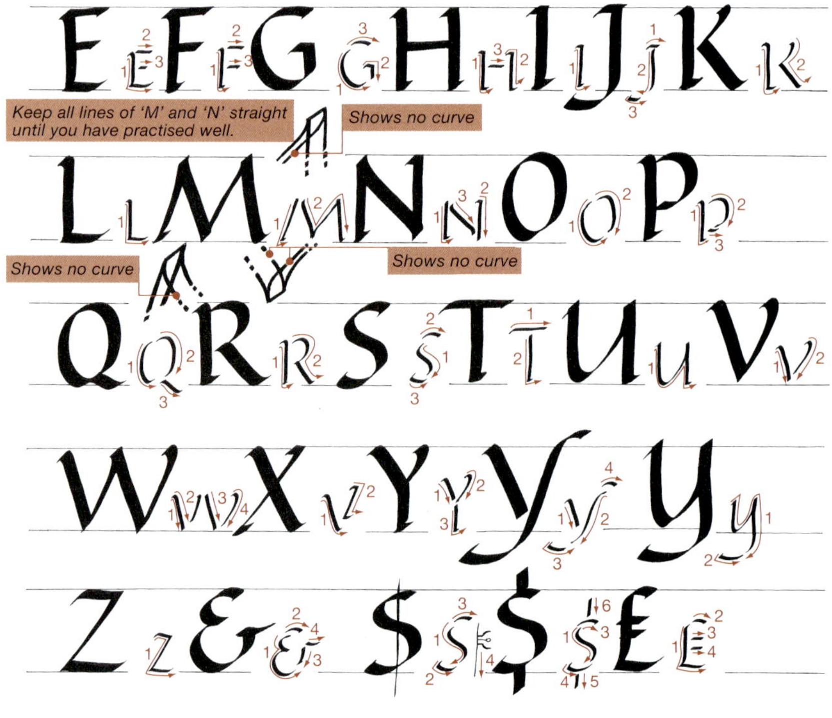

When you're learning a new calligraphy style and the letter shapes are coming naturally, try writing a small number of short words (for example, people's names), trying to keep the letters looking evenly spaced and sloped. Then write something a little longer, perhaps a saying, or an address. Italic is a useful script for many kinds of text, but it will take a lot of practice before you can evenly write a full page, like the one below. The original piece is about three times this height, and was written in blue and red **gouache** paint, using a William Mitchell Round Hand nib.

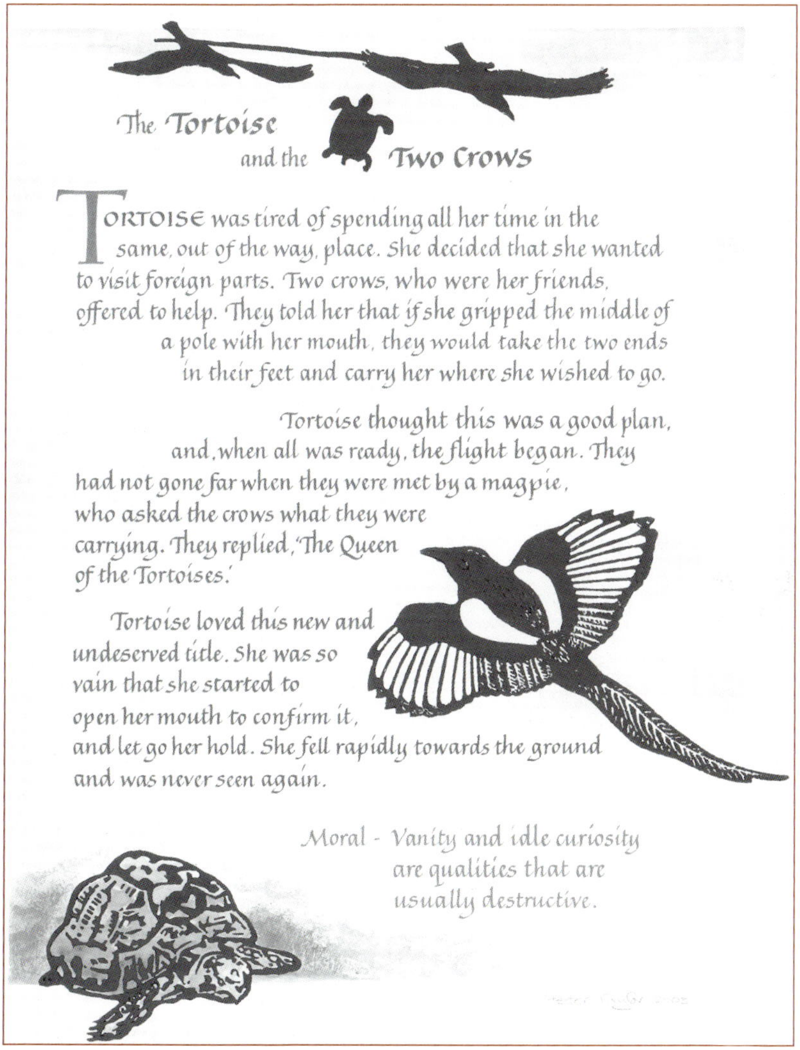

The Tortoise and the Two Crows

TORTOISE was tired of spending all her time in the same, out of the way, place. She decided that she wanted to visit foreign parts. Two crows, who were her friends, offered to help. They told her that if she gripped the middle of a pole with her mouth, they would take the two ends in their feet and carry her where she wished to go.

Tortoise thought this was a good plan, and, when all was ready, the flight began. They had not gone far when they were met by a magpie, who asked the crows what they were carrying. They replied, 'The Queen of the Tortoises.'

Tortoise loved this new and undeserved title. She was so vain that she started to open her mouth to confirm it, and let go her hold. She fell rapidly towards the ground and was never seen again.

Moral - Vanity and idle curiosity are qualities that are usually destructive.

Italic calligraphy by Peter Taylor

Uncial

This version of Uncial is actually a modernised version of Half-Uncials, which was originally a style that fell halfway between Uncials written all in capitals and an alphabet composed of capitals and small letters. It has retained many features of the scripts used in the **Book of Kells**, the **Lindisfarne Gospels** and other books written in about the 8th century. At that time, capitals used for headings and to start paragraphs were often entirely different or extremely ornate so new capitals have been designed to go with these small letters.

Writing Uncial calligraphy

The usual x-height of these Uncial letters is 4½ nib-widths. Though some letters like 'b' and 'l' can be sloped, it is generally a vertical alphabet and the pen is maintained at a constant angle of your choice between 0° and 10°. The shape of all letters is controlled by the shape of the 'o'. The centre of the pen nib follows a circle, so the inside shape is narrower than a perfect circle and the outside is wider. It's often easiest to think about where the centre of the nib is moving while you write, or watch the white space inside the **counter** of letters as you create it.

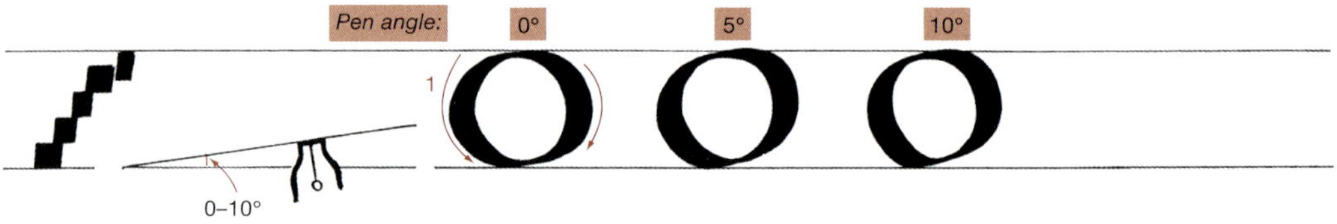

One of the features of these letters is the big triangular serif.

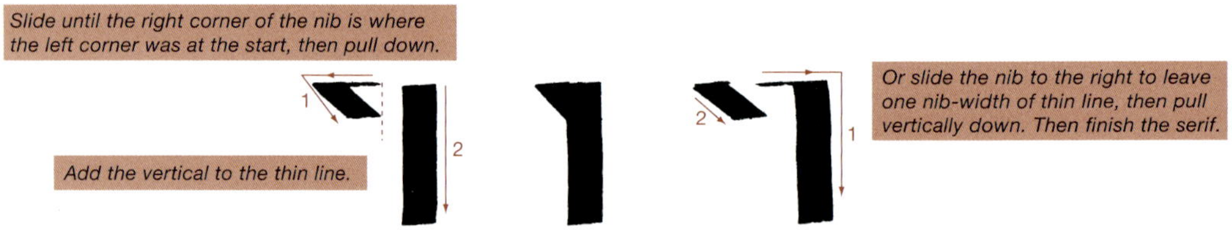

On some letters of the alphabet on the next page, like 'f', 'p', 'r' and 'q', I've chosen to make the serif below the top guideline and the curved part of each letter grow from it or on to it.

Here's the complete alphabet.

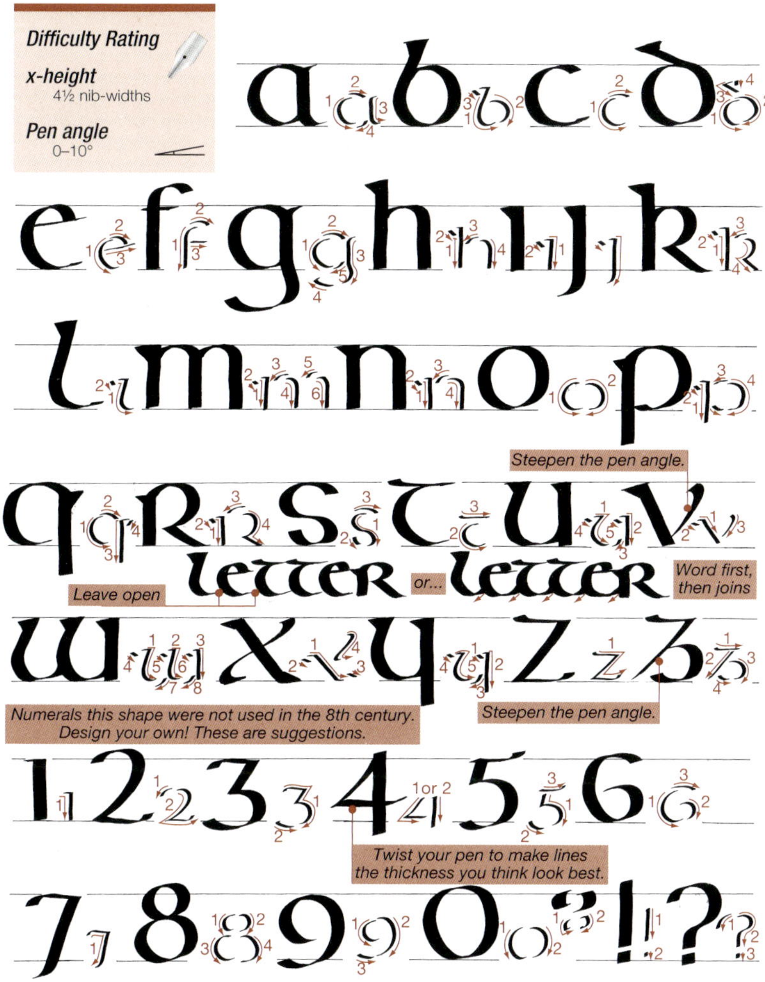

Originally, the lower end of a vertical stroke was wider than the top, due to the monks pressing harder on the quill and making the nib splay. If you would like to add this feature to letters, you can pull the nib a little to the left when you get close to the line, then add another stroke on the right:

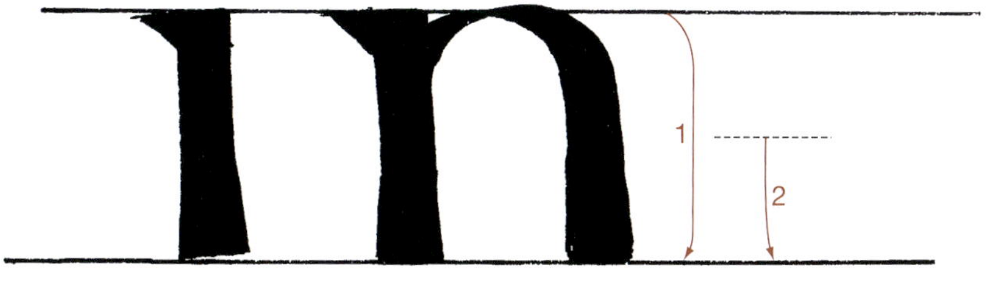

Many of these modernised capitals are large versions of the small letters. The serifs on 'T' and 'Z' were partially drawn by pulling the wet ink on the letter into shape with the corner of the nib. The same technique can be used to shape the serif on 'D', if necessary. But you can twist your nib to create them any way you like.

Difficulty Rating

Letter Height
5½–6 nib-widths

Pen angle
Mainly 0°–10° with changes

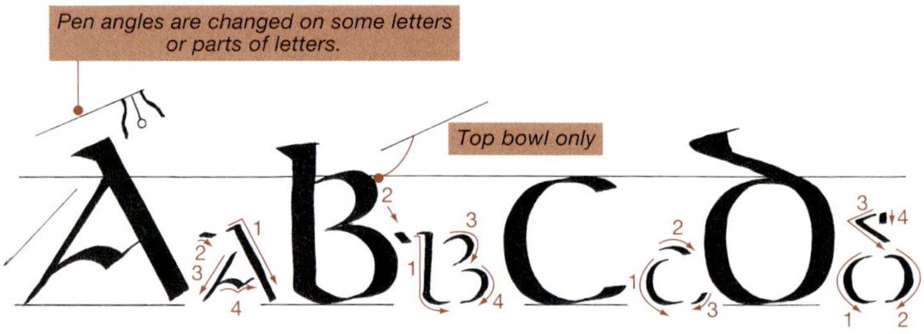

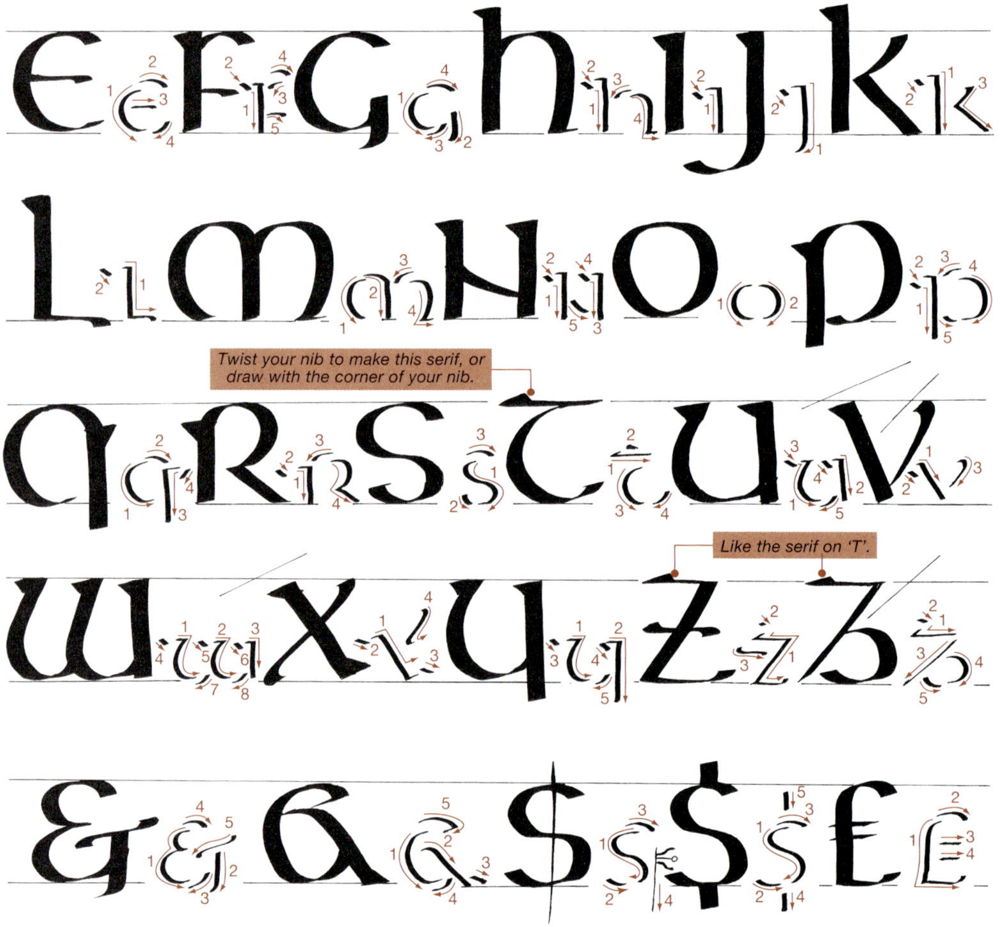

Forth from his den

to steal he stole

his bags of chink he chunk

And many a wicked

smile he smole

And many a wink he wunk

The above example of Uncial calligraphy shows the smallest size I usually write this script. It always takes up a lot of room. The bottom piece was written nearly three times the size it appears here. Colour has been added inside some letters, leaving a small space around the edge. As you can see, you don't have to write everything in straight lines. Don't be afraid to experiment! If adding dots to 'i's, I draw them as thin lines, but you can make them whatever shape you wish.

The long-maned croc and the wombadool

like to keep their tummies cool.

They stand in mud all day and night

And laugh and sing with all their might

Squidge, slop, blurp, glop...

... hee hee!

Creative and Decorative Letters

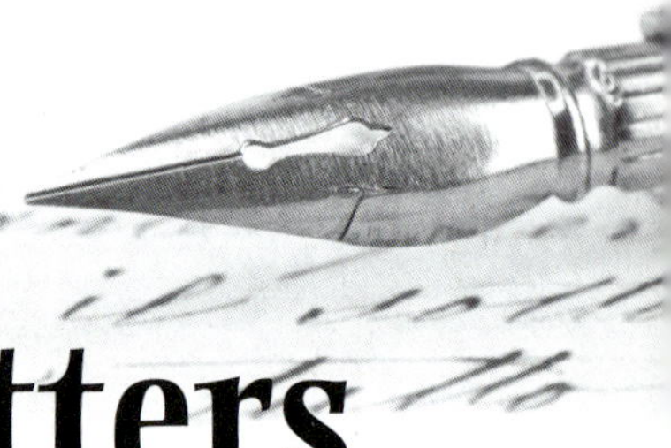

LETTERS CAN BE designed to create many special effects. Added details and patterns can make individual feature letters for starting the first paragraph of a long piece of writing or to create a title that stands out. Loops and flourishes on letters draw attention to the words on which they appear. It's a good idea to use them sparingly, but they're useful for emphasis and you can impress people with your skill. Decorating letters can also be fun! A framed decorated letter, or one made into a bookmark, for example, can become a treasured gift.

> **AUTHOR'S NOTE**
> I have used paint to produce many illustrations, but you'll still achieve very pleasing results if you use coloured pencils or felt-tip pens, which are much easier.

Modern versal letters

Though they could be coloured with pencils, felt pen or painted, the shapes of this variety of versal letters results from drawing them with calligraphy pens and changing the pen angle for different strokes – but you should understand and practise the other varieties before attempting these.

> ***Difficulty Rating***
>
> ***Letter height***
> About 17 nib-widths
>
> ***Pen angle***
> Mainly 30° and 10°, but many more changes, too.

All letter parts have two overlapping pen strokes. It is hard to make elements a similar width on different letters.

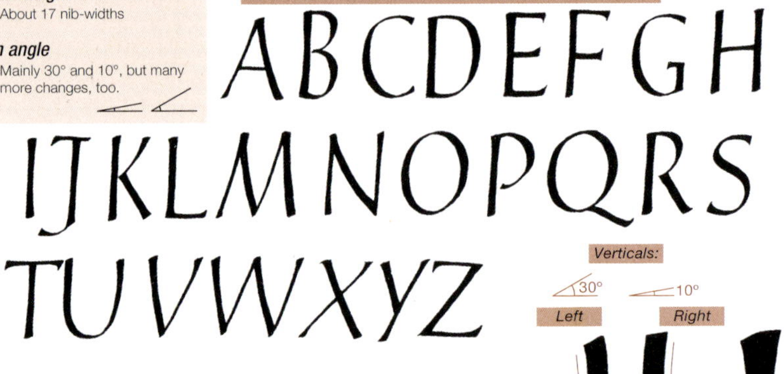

Note: Serifs are drawn at many angles, each using a different pen angle.

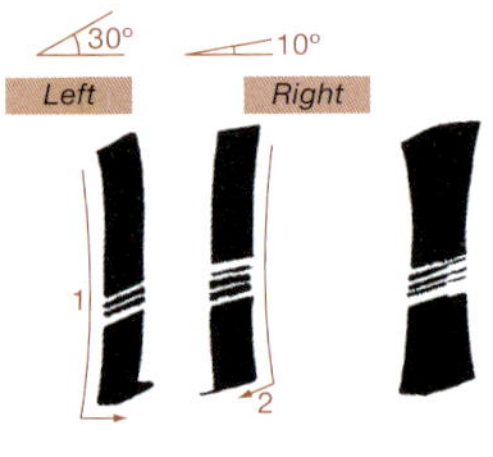

Decorating pen-made letters

Decorations can be added to pen-written letters, too. You can keep an alphabet with all its normal features – the ones that make it look good – but then add some extras, as per the following examples.

Spirals

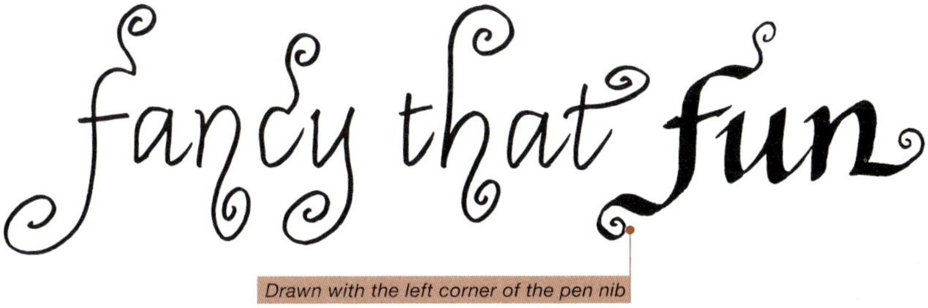

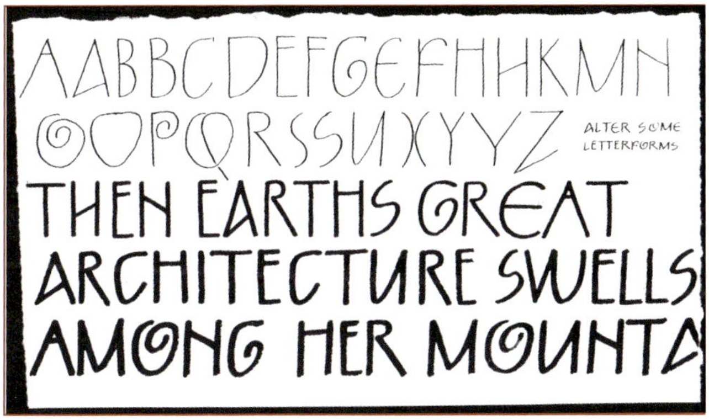

Using decorative letters, calligraphy by Olive Bull.

Hearts

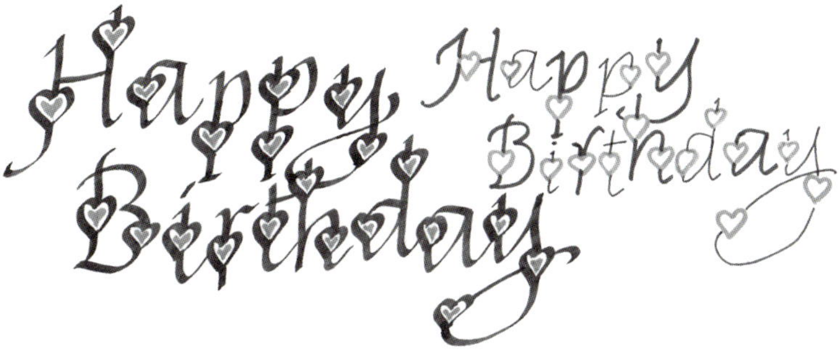

Flourishes and more

Here are the flourish designs I use a lot when I'm writing people's names on certificates or invitations. For that kind of work, I only put **flourishes** on the bottoms of letters. Remember, not all letters can have flourishes added.

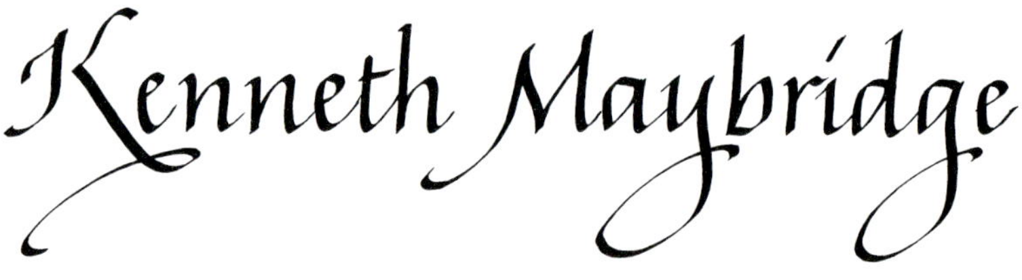

You can see that the flourishes are much bigger than the height of the '**bowl**' part – often five times the size, or even more.

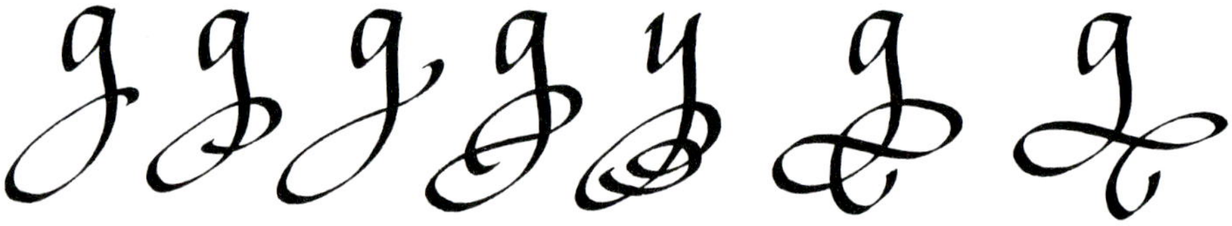

Though I've used a calligraphy pen, you can make flourishes with any writing tool and for letters of almost all handwriting styles.

I've written most of these shapes on 'g's, but you could use any of them as the tail of a 'y', and on 'p', but for that letter, 'p', you would have to have the straight part of the tail on the normal slope of the tail of a 'p', not gently 's' shaped, like these 'g's and the 'y'.

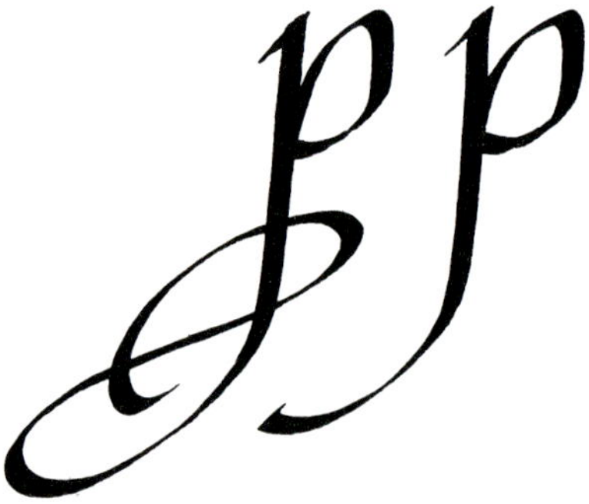

If you want to get really technical, here is what makes a letter 'g' or 'y' elegant in any style, whether it's had flourishes added or not.

From the 'bowl' part, make the tail line go straight, like all other letters, until it almost reaches the bottom line.

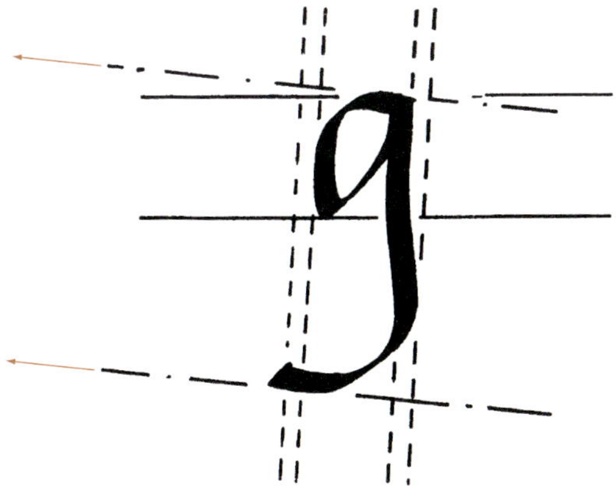

As you carry on drawing the tail, make it swing just a tiny bit out to the right as you go down, then imagine your pen is a car and you're driving a quarter of the way around a very large roundabout. In other words, swing that line in a big and very generous curve – no kinks in the corner.

If you are not going to add flourishes to the letter, keep the bottom almost flat, but pointing slightly uphill (as per the example shown above). I make the top of the bowl and the flat part at the bottom of the tail parallel to each other.

However much you swing the tail out from the right-hand side of the letter, the left-hand corner of the tail must be at least that width to the left-hand side of the left edge of the letter.

When there are two 'g's, 'y's or 'p's together, it's usually best to only add flourishes to the first one. The same applies when you write two letter 'f's together – give the second one a shorter, simpler tail, but start the second 'f' higher than the first one.

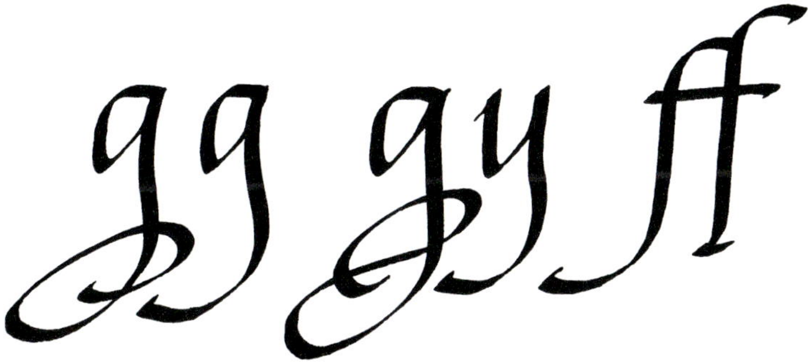

Here are some other tips for making flourishes look good:

1. Make lines cross over each other to create big spaces. Don't make several lines meet at the same place or the results looks blobby.

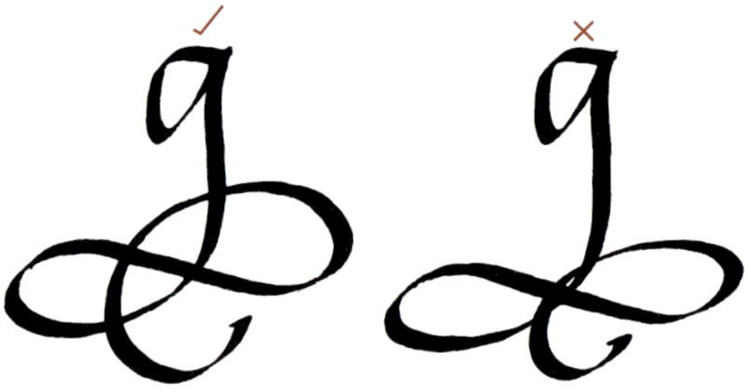

2. For the best and most eye-pleasing result, when you get to the end of your flourish, as you lift your hand from the paper, keep drawing in mid-air either a spiral or a figure-8 shape (which could be on its side or at an angle).

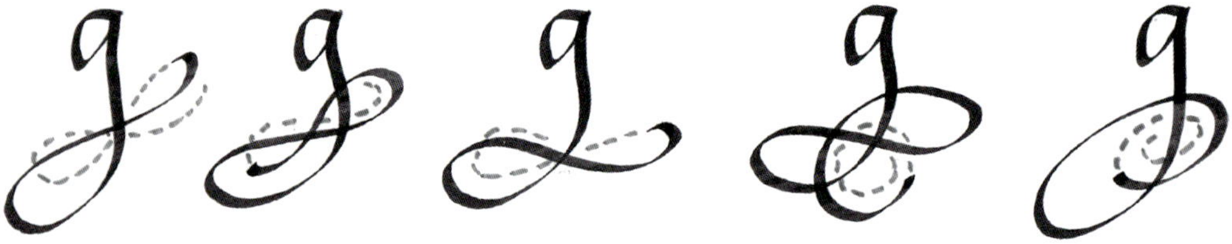

If you look at calligraphy books, or work that has been done by experts, you'll find lots of different ways to add flourishes to letters. Some you'll like more than others.

If you think a flourish shape looks hard to do, or you want to draw one that you see in a book, the easiest way to learn the shape is to carefully trace over an example 10 times, then do one for yourself, freehand. Trace the original another 10 times and do one for yourself, freehand. Trace another 10 times – and when you do the next one freehand, it will be just about perfect.

Donald Jackson, the **Queen's scribe** since 1964, was one of my teachers. In our first class, he drew a fancy letter 'A' on the board, something like the example on the right, and said, 'Now you do one.'

As you can imagine, we were all horrified.

'It's easy,' he said, and smiled. 'An eight-year-old child can do it!' And he made us point at the board and follow the line many times with our finger, then draw a letter.

Can you do one? I've shown you where to start and what order to do the strokes. Try the 'carefully trace × 10 (in mid-air, if you wish), one freehand, trace × 10, freehand, trace × 10' method and see how close your last one is to mine when you again write it freehand.

Be proud of yourself when they become easy!

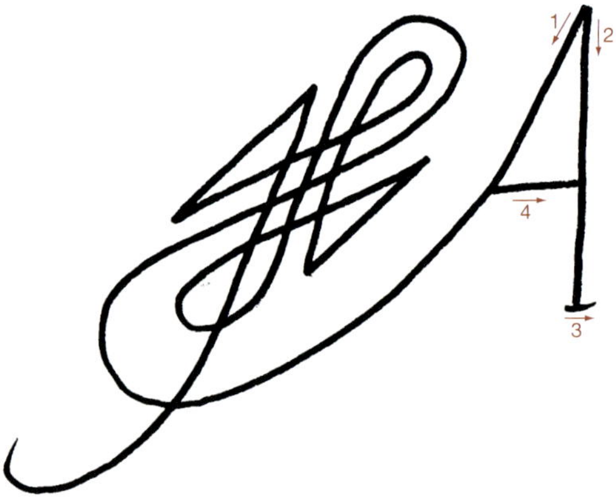

There are many simpler ways to add decorative features to Italic capital letters.

A B C D E F G

You could use different colours for the letters, lines and diamonds.

H I J K L M

A small gold or white dot inside the diamonds is also effective.

N O P Q R S

T U V W X Y Z

A B C D E F G

You may need to change your pen angle or twist the paper around to add some of the diamonds.

H I J K L M

N O P Q R S

T U V W X Y Z

Keep flourishes generous but not overdone

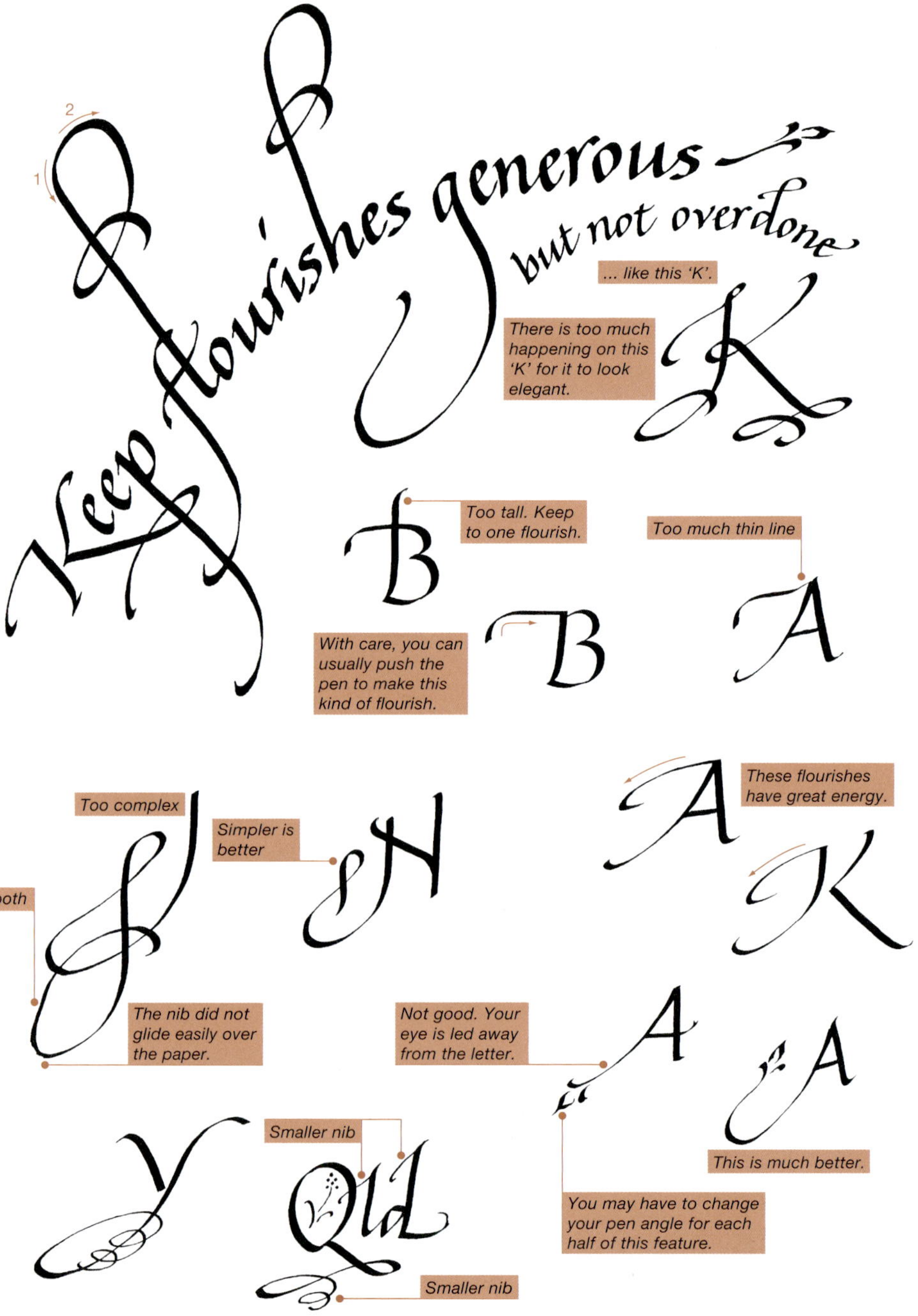

Only occasionally will I add flourishes to the tops of letters. Then, it's usually for a decorative name, heading or title, but you can use them on the top line of writing if it's something important.

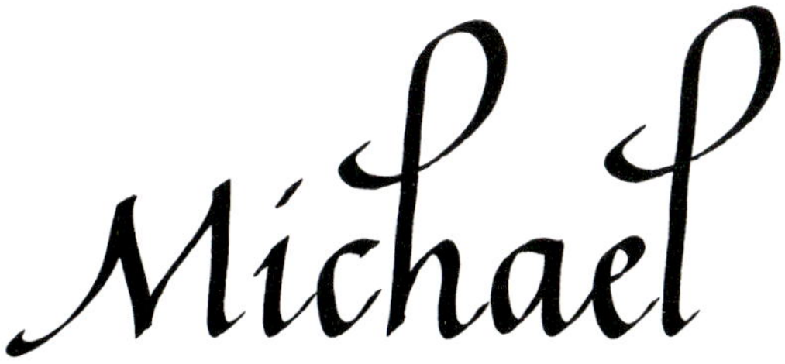

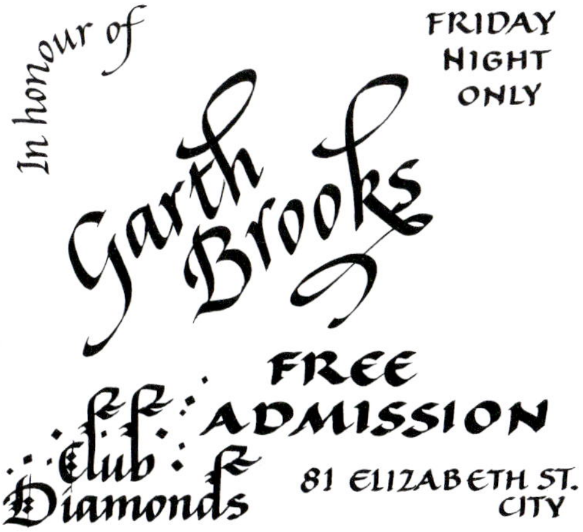

It can make people feel special when they see their name with flourishes. Flourishes say 'Look at me!' Can you see what's wrong in this Garth Brooks advert? Yes, the flourishes on the word 'Club' slope backwards and don't match the slope of other letters. Though we all make errors of judgement from time to time, flourishes make them stand out!

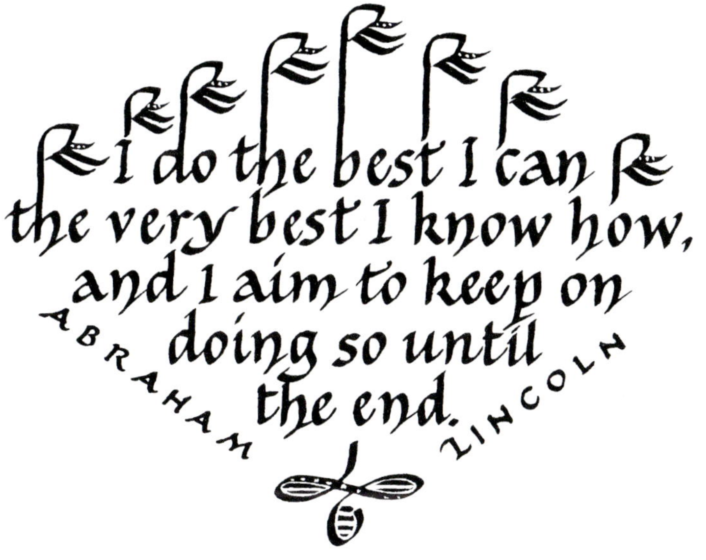

Can you guess what colours have been used for this quotation? The small letters and ascenders, plus the top stroke of each flourish are blue. The bottom two strokes are red, so that the flourishes look like a line of US flags. White dots have been added to represent the flags' stars. As a contrast and to almost complete a red border around the saying, Abraham Lincoln has also been written in red. This artwork is about the size of the original.

The next set of examples shows you some good and easy ways to add flourishes to the tops of letters. You can use these flourishes for decorating the tops of any tall letters but you might need to make them five times higher than usual – and remember, these designs are only good for writing titles, the top lines of some writing, or for special purposes.

Start with a very small rounded hook. Cut most of it off when you add a long S shape without a top or bottom. Add shapes like hearts cut in half.

Alternatively, you can add skateboard or ski shapes at the end, or loops or spirals. Remember the rule – for the nicest finishing shape, keep your pen moving in a spiral or a figure-8 pattern when you lift it from the paper.

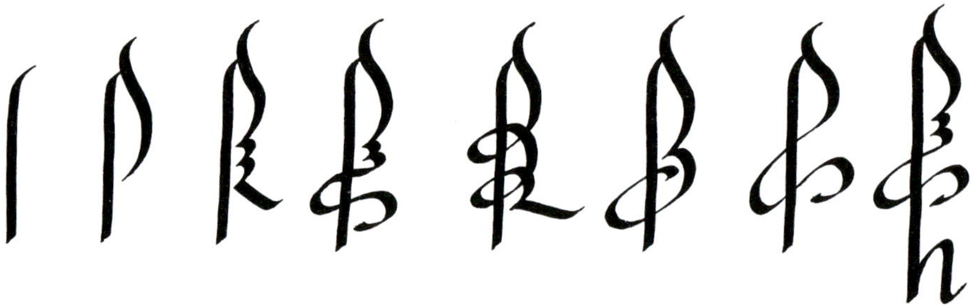

It's usually a good idea to put some lined paper under your working sheet so that you can see where to aim, or lightly draw pencil lines with the aid of a ruler and erase them later. Always write the letters freehand.

It's probably best to keep flourishes angular for Gothic writing styles, and add **hackles**, diamonds or fine lines if you wish.

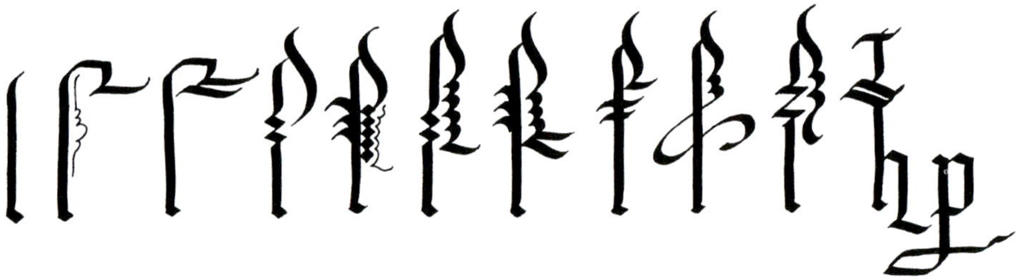

You don't need to add flourishes to every tall letter in a line of writing. If you want a pattern of flourishes, you can aim one at the side of almost any letter, and leave a gap, but be careful that you don't aim one at the side of an 'a' and make it look like a 'd', or at the side of an 'n' and make it look like an 'h'.

Similarly, you can aim bottom flourishes at letters, without touching, and likewise, you have to make sure that you don't make a letter 'u' look like a 'y'.

When I am adding loops to the tops of letters, I start the letter as normal, but then turn the paper upside down to draw on the loops, as if I were decorating a 'g' or 'y'.

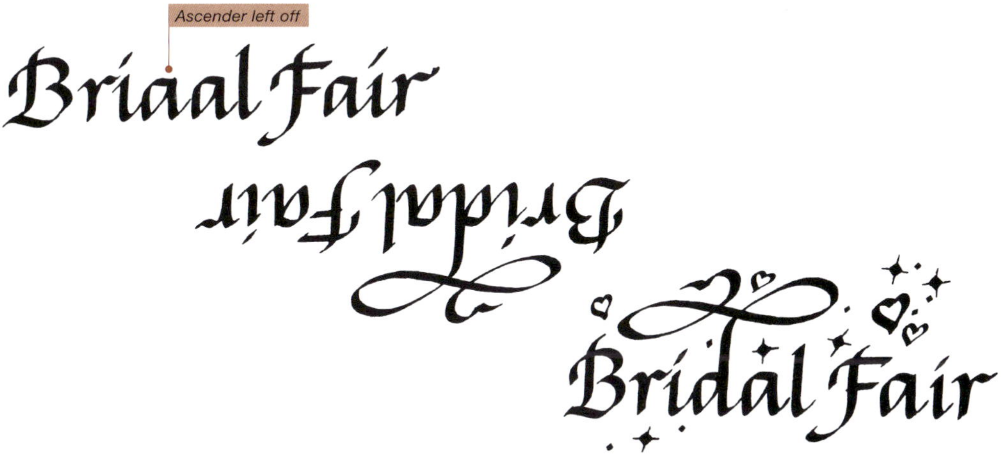

Cadel capitals

Cadel capitals were initially used to accompany Bâtarde Gothic and Rotunda letters. There are innumerable variations, so I'll just show you the concept to enable you to copy any you see that you like, or to make up your own. These capitals are best initially drawn with a pencil to plan them out and the lines then written over in pen and ink.

The spine is drawn first, then loops, spurs and boxes added. Always make feet (replacements for serifs) less detailed and lighter weight than the main letter parts. Gaps can be filled in with flowers or other designs and a pointed or fine pen used to add hair-thickness lines and small details.

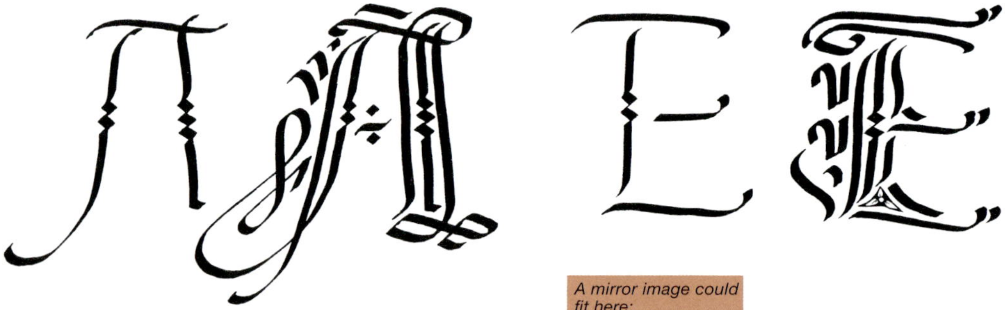

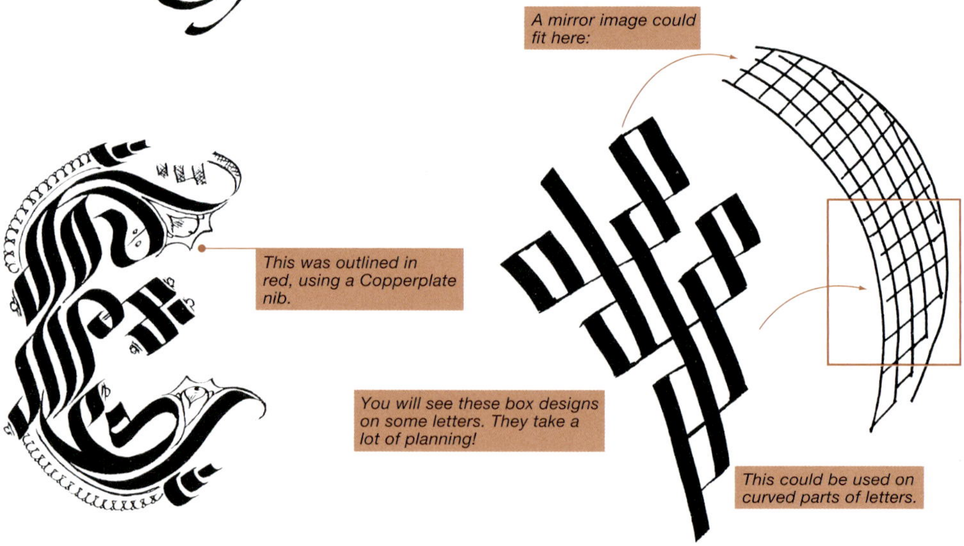

Possible parts of Cadel capitals

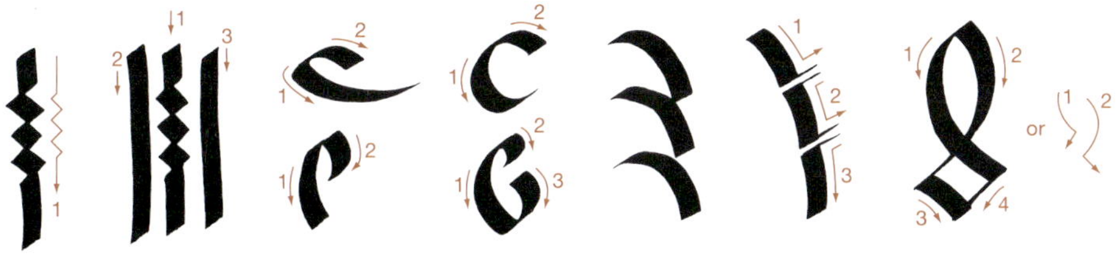

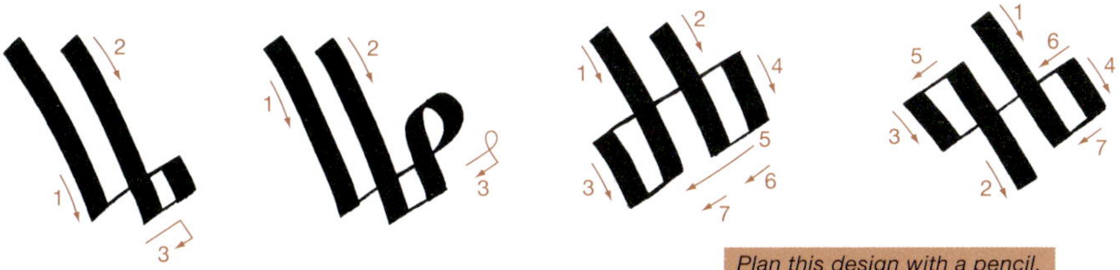

Plan this design with a pencil, then draw over it.

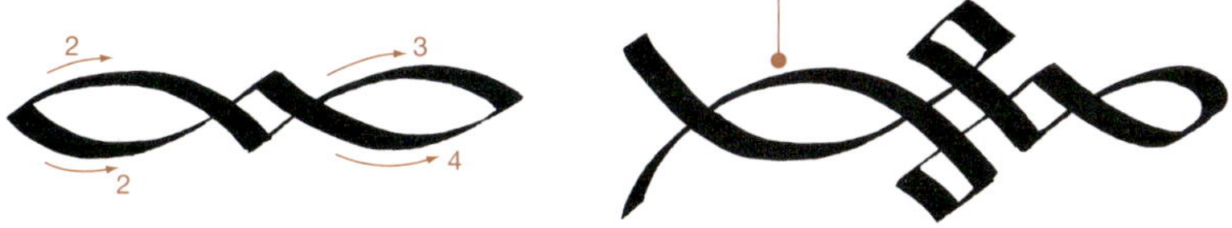

You may find it easier to use different stroke orders.

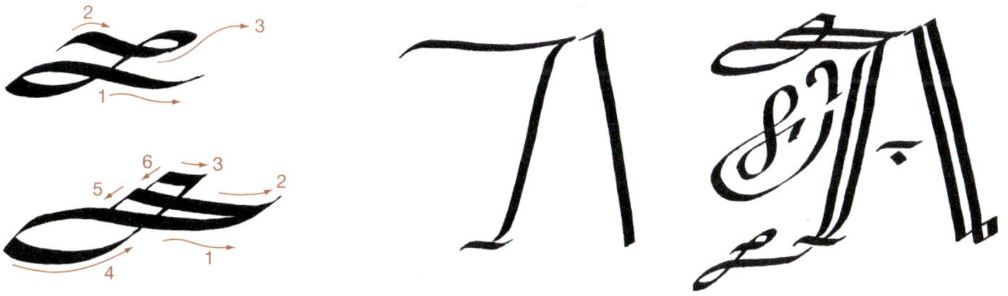

Plan designs in pencil, then start in the middle and work outwards.

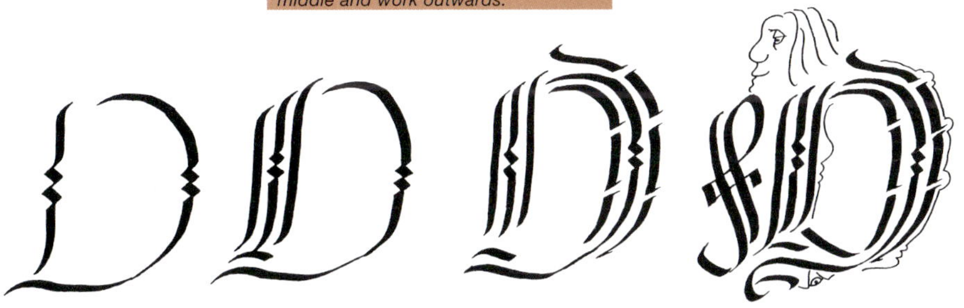

Designing Letters

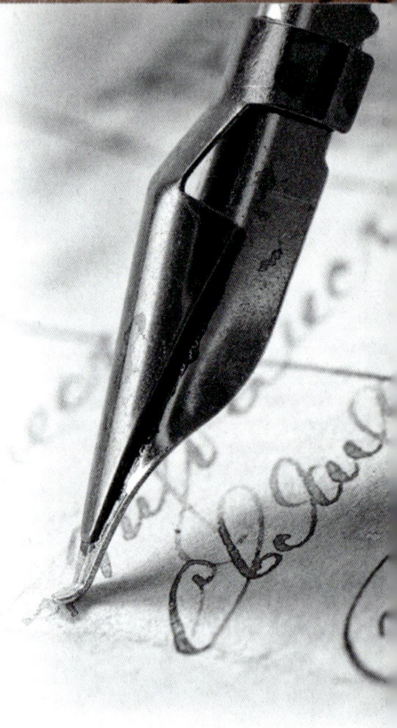

DESIGNING LETTERS IS a really fun thing to do! You can enjoy letting your imagination run wild, like this:

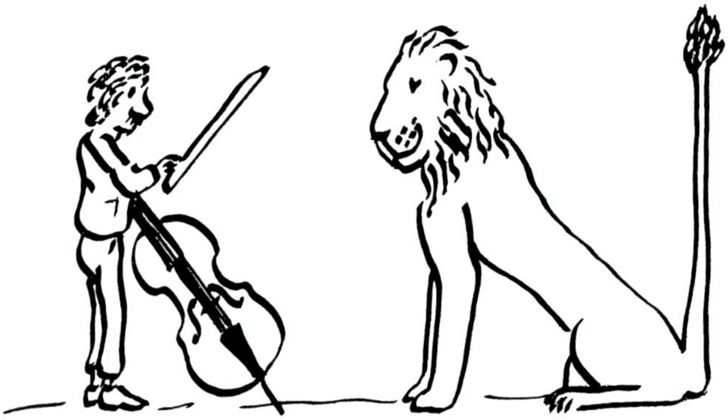

...but I guess these don't really qualify as calligraphic letters.

Calligraphy doesn't mean that everything has to be smooth and perfect. The proportions of the calligraphic letters below closely resemble the original carved Roman capitals, even though they appear to be scribbled.

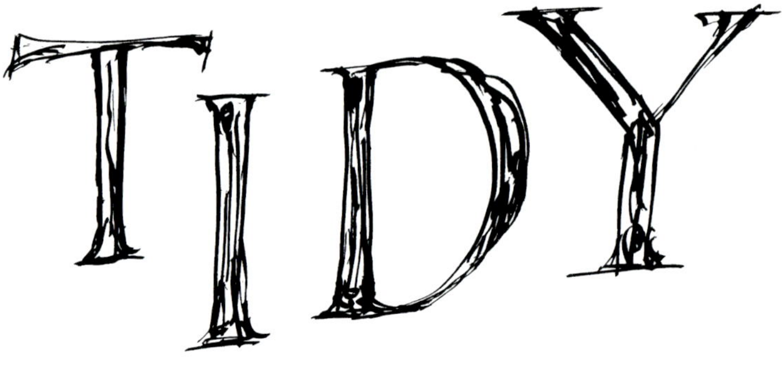

In this delightful painting by Nathalie Tousnakhoff, all curved letter parts have a rounded shape and the accepted rules for elegant letters are followed. For example, the bottoms of 'k' and 'R' are wider than the tops, the tail of 'g' balances the bowl above it and the upper part of 's' encloses less space than the bottom. These features make the letters pleasing to the eye.

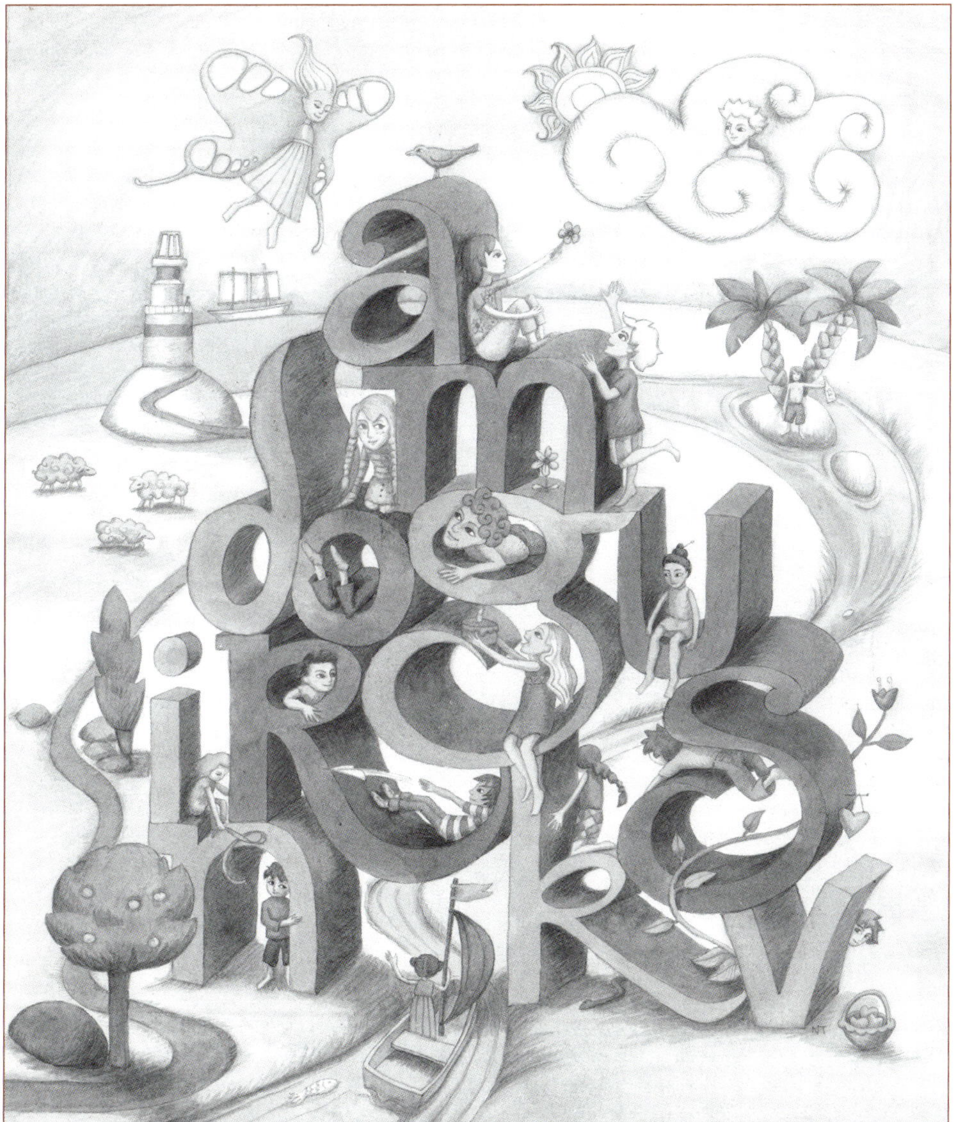

From 'Petites histoires d'amour qui tournent court', éditions Chocolat Jeunesse, 2010, calligrapher and artist Nathalie Tousnakhoff

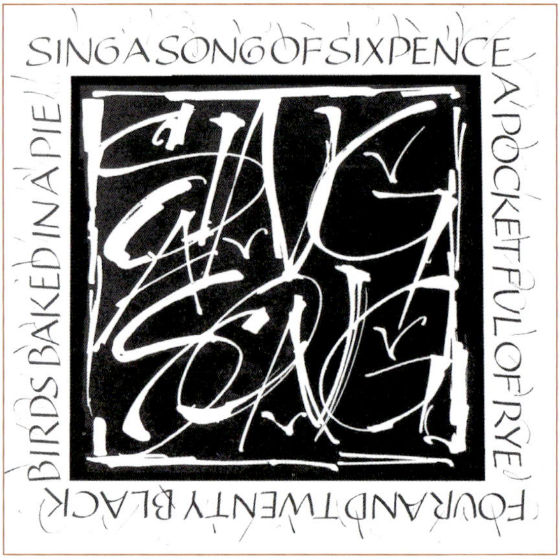

Calligraphy by Colleen Little

In every book on calligraphy, you'll read that for normal scripts, all letters in an alphabet should relate to the shape, slope and width of the letter 'o'. Circular 'o' in Foundational Hand leads to the use of circular tops to other letters, the thinnest point tells us what pen angle should be maintained, the vertical 'n' sets the slope and, together with 'i', the serif structures are used throughout. The area inside the 'o' also controls the width of 'n', other letters and their spacing.

So if I gave you some letters such as the ones below, I'm sure you could design the rest of each alphabet just using the features drawn. The pen angle and nature of the letters will also help you to add a dot to the i's – should it be circular, a square, comma, thin line or doesn't it matter?

AUTHOR'S NOTE

In any alphabet the letter 'k' is always wider at the bottom than at the top.

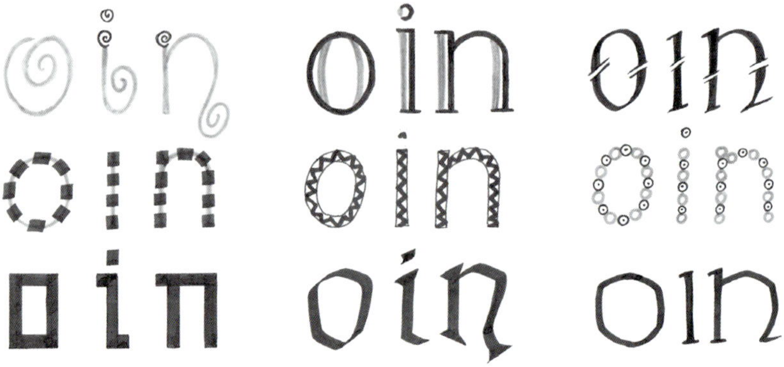

Designing Lively Gothic and other Gothic variations

Let's try to build a new family of Lively Gothic letters. We'll still use the 'o' shape to control width and keep it vertical, but change a couple of features on 'n' to make it more lively. Then, again, we'll build all the other letters from these two.

The variety of corner structures provides extra interest.

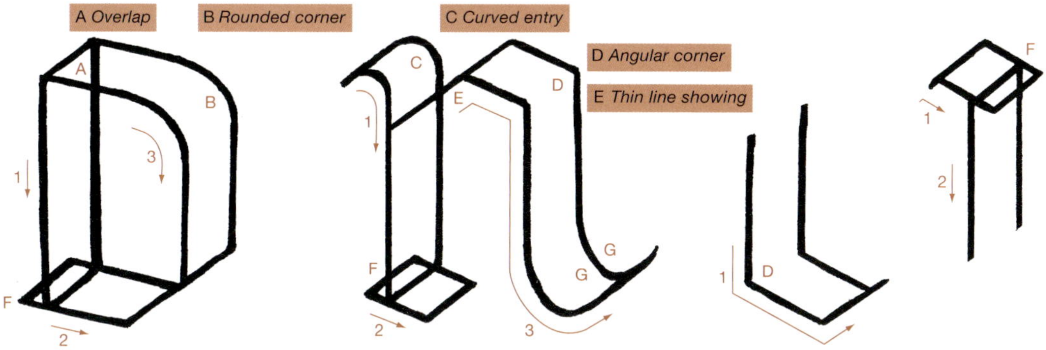

F *The pen is removed from the paper and repositioned before the next stroke is started.*
G *Curved exit stroke. This and other rounded elements give the script extra life.*

Practise a simple Gothic alphabet before trying this one.

Difficulty Rating

x-height
5–6 nib-widths

Pen angle
About 40°

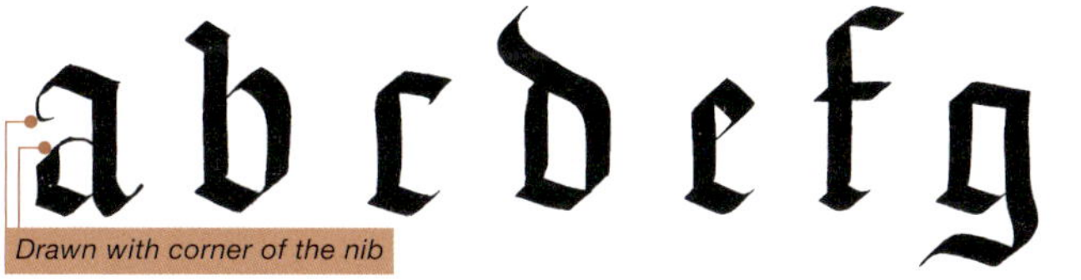

Drawn with corner of the nib

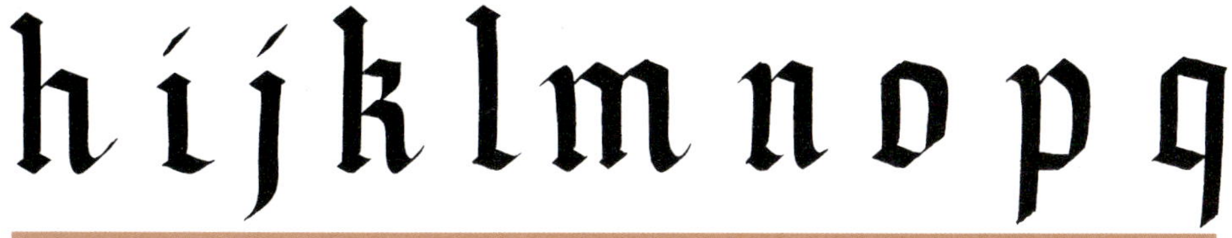

Numerals as we know them today were not in use when alphabets similar to this were developed in the 14th century.

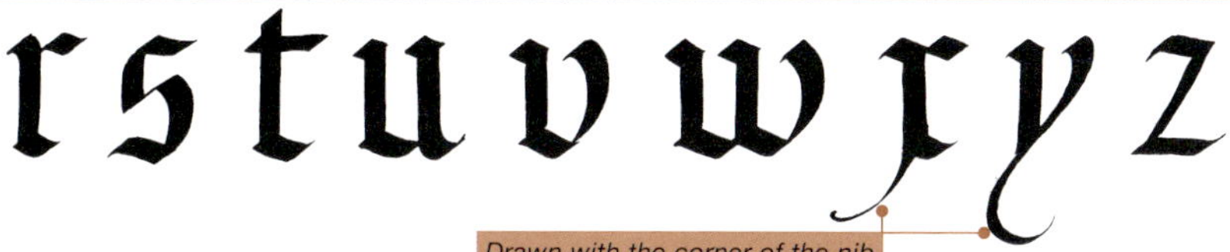

Drawn with the corner of the nib

Here is a suggestion for related capitals that could accompany the script on page 47.

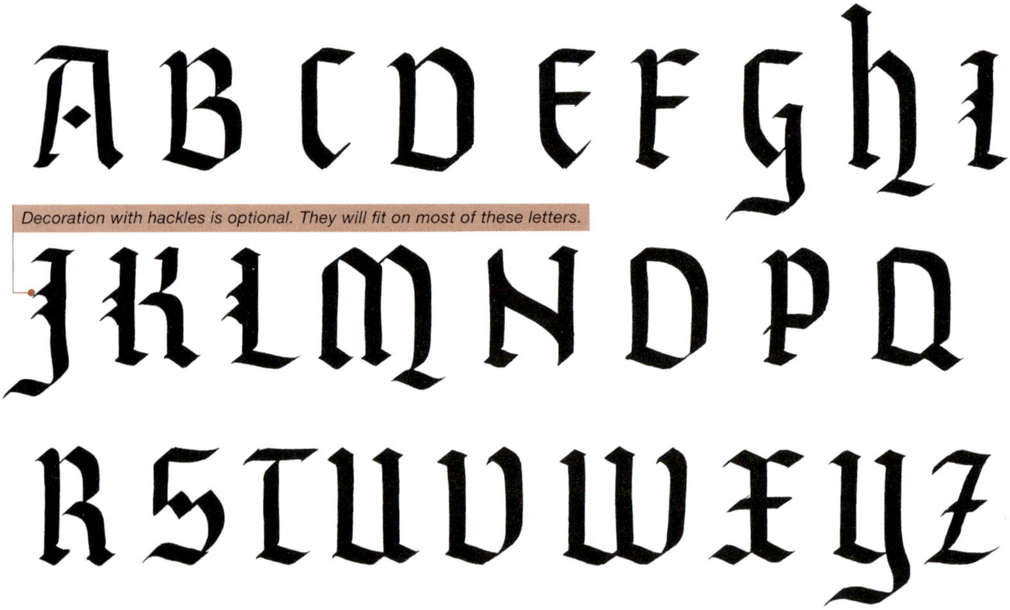

Decoration with hackles is optional. They will fit on most of these letters.

This works well with small letter sizes, but may not be as effective if written large – I'll leave it to your personal taste. The following are some other Gothic variations.

Practise a simple version of Gothic before trying this one.

Difficulty Rating

x-height
5–6 nib-widths

Pen angle
About 40°

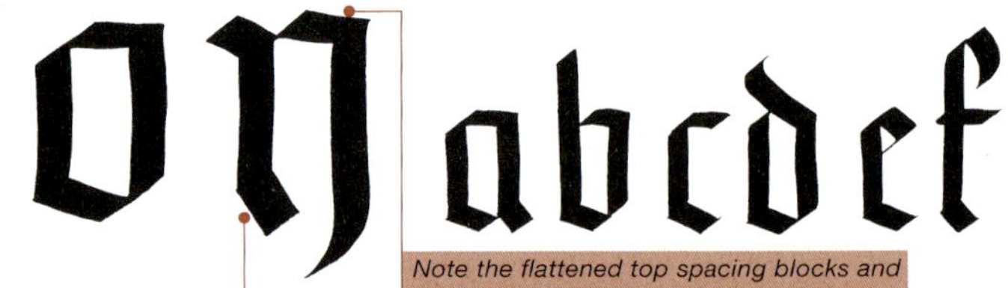

Note the flattened top spacing blocks and steeply sloping bottom serifs.

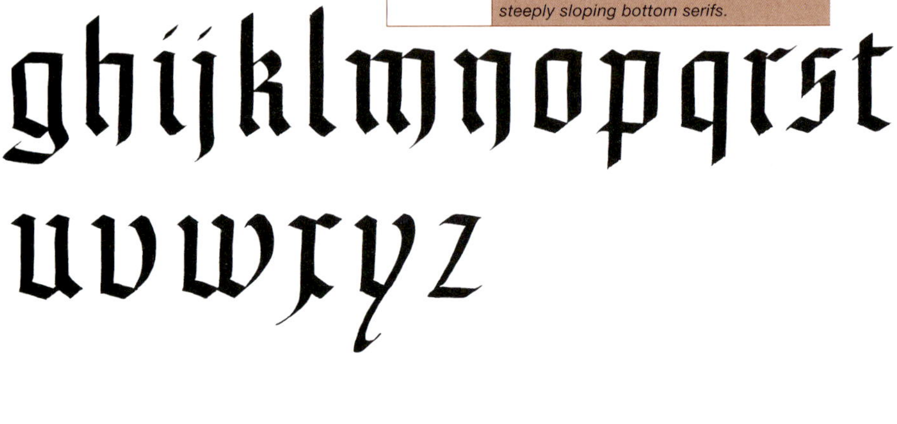

This alphabet is based on 'Rounded Gothic', previously described. The bottom joining point (x) no longer lines up with the top corner (y).

Difficulty Rating

x-height
5 nib-widths

Pen angle
Not less than 45°

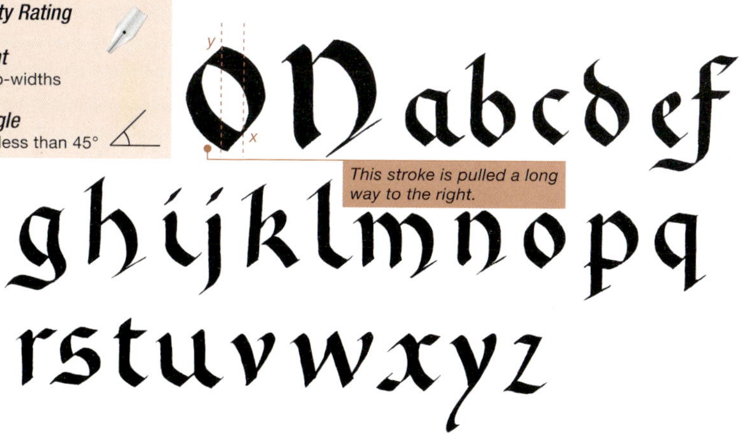

Changing Italic

When Italic is written at speed, slope is naturally increased and exit strokes get longer. It can be made into handwriting, but most calligraphy is separate from handwriting. Handwriting is vibrant, but it looks too casual for something that is 'important'. If people are paying a calligrapher to write for them, they expect the job to be done in something more than just neat handwriting.

There are many ways Italic can be re-designed to suit your own preference or the kind of text you're working on. Italic is made more formal by keeping exit strokes short, using more precise and restrained serif structures, and fewer decorative flourishes and flamboyant touches to ascenders and descenders.

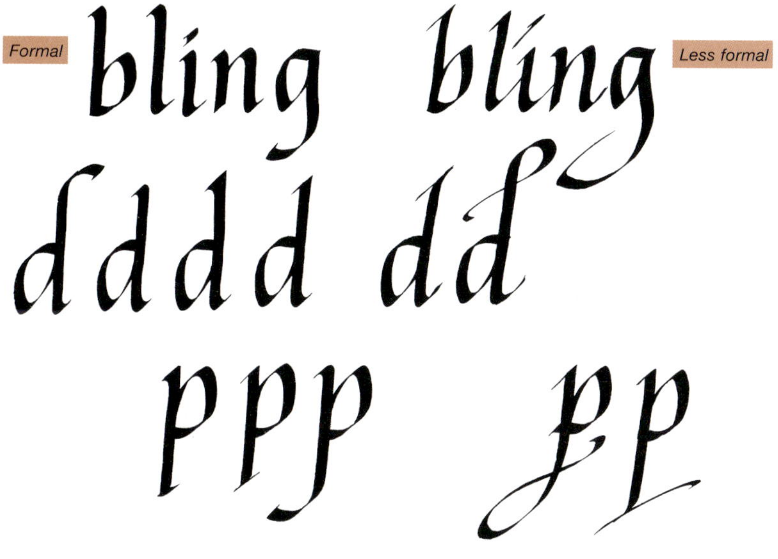

Designing Lively Foundational Hand with Italic features

You can create new styles by adding Italic features to other alphabets, such as Foundational Hand, as **Irene Wellington** did in the middle of the 1900s. The writing below is my version of her script with many letters having fluid Italic style exit strokes while other features have the strength of Foundational. We'll call it Lively Foundational.

The North wind doth blow
and we shall have snow
And what will poor
robin do then, poor thing

Take a look at the letters below. Though slightly compressed and sloping, the 'o' has a rounded top and bottom. This gives the Foundational-style top to 'n' and a generous rounded nature to 'b' and 'p'. Because the arches are obviously constructed as separate letter strokes (unlike branching Italic arches), their structure helps our eyes to recognise the care that's gone into the writing in this style. The separate strokes of 's', 'w', 'k' and 'f' build on this. The rounded Foundational entry and exit strokes of the first limb of 'n' give the alphabet a degree of formality. Its foot is firmly planted on the line – it's got strength to stand up – but the second limb is different. It has a bouncy curved Italic style exit with a **hairline** that leads to the next letter.

o n b p s w k f

This Italic-style exit and extended hairline give the letters life, but they are not just casually written. The downstroke of 'n' (see below) is stopped for a fraction of a second when it hits the **baseline**, and then the fine exit stroke is almost flicked off the bottom of that part of the letter. It's used on many other letters to give them a family resemblance.

Irene Wellington may well have used a **quill** for her writing, and twisted it on to its corner to construct these fine lines. You can get the idea and the same feel by using two pencils taped together to write with like a pen. Ensure both points remain on the paper until the bottom of the appropriate stroke is reached, then stop, keeping the left-hand pencil point on the paper, but twist the pencils to lift off the right-hand point. Draw the curved exit stroke with the left-hand pencil (which would normally be the corner of the pen nib).

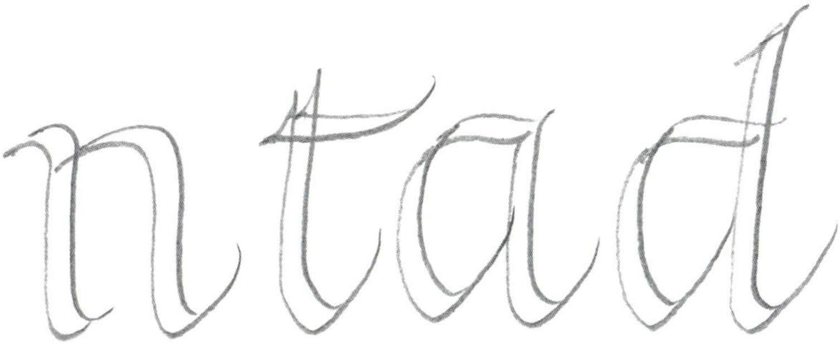

Exit strokes drawn with the 'nib' corner

Irene added the fine tweaks on the tops of 's's this way, too. You may or may not be able to use your pen the same way but it's worth giving it a try. If the flow of ink in your pen won't let you do this, it will still look good if you use normal sliding strokes to create 'a', 'd' and other letters and their exits.

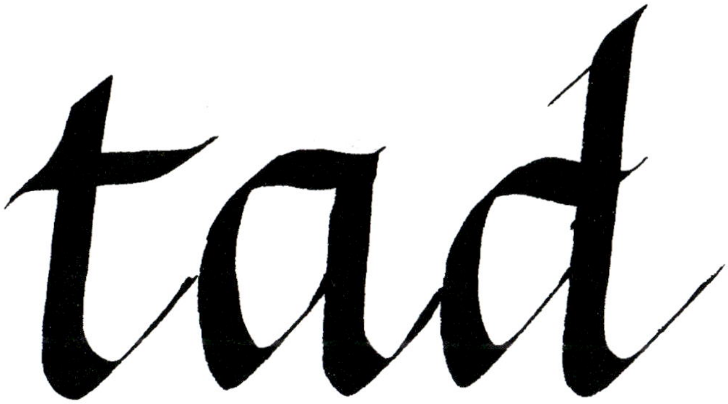

Sliding exit strokes

The fine serif line on the tops of ascenders indicates care in letter construction to please the eye. Extra life and flavour is added to the letters of the alphabet by not just using a simple tick up and down but by taking the pen off the paper after the upwards 'tick', doing a tiny loop in mid-air, then planting the nib back on the paper to start the thick stroke. This should begin with a curved entry and the tiniest of curved points at the top right-hand corner. The tick joins will appear to join on to the letter at a point somewhere on this curved entry into the vertical.

With 'e' written in two strokes with a fine swished exit at the top, and curved comma shaped dots on 'i' and 'j', the calligrapher's enjoyment in writing is also shared by the reader.

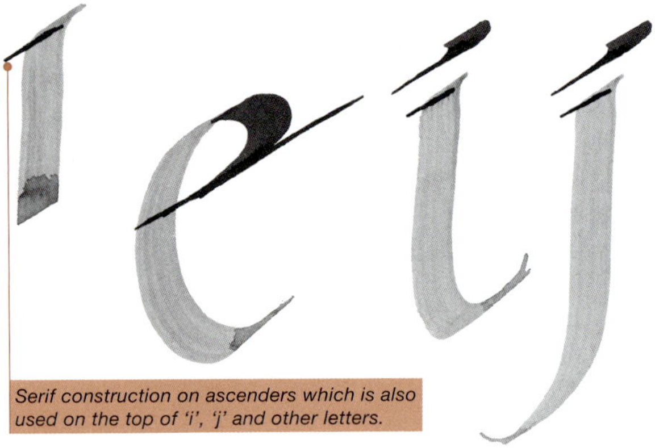

Serif construction on ascenders which is also used on the top of 'i', 'j' and other letters.

Gaining confidence

Once you've practised the 'basic' calligraphy styles of Foundational/ Roman, Uncial, Gothic and Italic, and written a good number of things in them, you'll develop enough confidence so that you no longer have to think about what shape each letter should be and how you need to construct it. Those things will come automatically. You'll also find that using a pen is as natural as pointing with your finger and you will know exactly what thickness line is going to result as you draw with it, change pen angles and play around.

Keeping family resemblances between letter shapes in an alphabet, and relating them all to the shape of 'o', 'i' and 'n', ensures a pleasing result when words are written, but each calligrapher's version of any alphabet is unique. In a small town with only a few calligraphers, it's easy to look at signs in shops, names on place cards at weddings or restaurant menus, like the one opposite, and recognise who has written them. One of the design features that calligraphers consciously or subconsciously change is the structure of serifs. Others are the **weight** of the letters – how high each letter is in terms of pen-widths – and the length of ascenders and descenders.

For much of their writing, most calligraphers, after a short while, will no longer draw a top guideline. For a particular style and pen size, letter size will be automatically written at a natural desired height and will be a personal design feature.

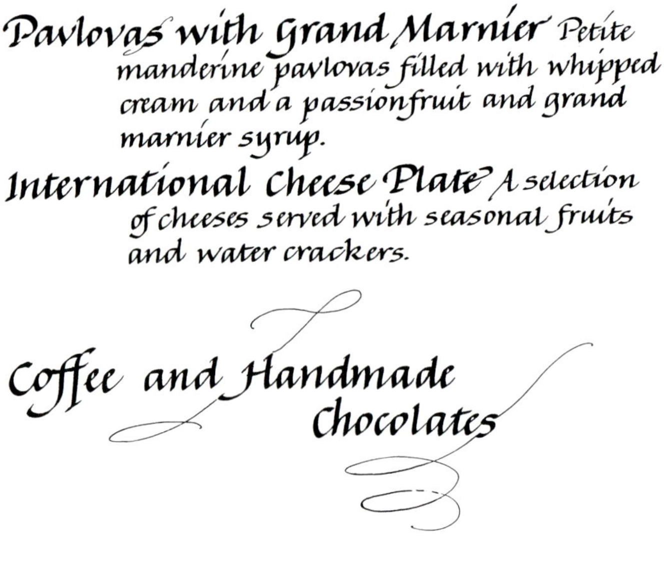

Copying styles you like

In this book and in others, you'll probably find examples of people's work with letter shapes that you'd like to copy or at least use to develop something that looks similar. To help you along, try figuring out the following features of the original work:

- the height of letters in nib-widths
- the slope of letters
- the shape of an 'o', 'i' and 'n', in particular, so that other letters can have similar features
- the normal pen angle and any parts of letters where the pen angle has been changed
- serif structures
- the probable order in which the strokes were made
- how quickly you think the letters were written (fast, medium, slow, extremely slow)
- the size of the letters (sometimes a picture will have a note under it that tells you the size of the artwork)
- what kind of writing tool and surface was used (again, accompanying notes sometimes tell you this, or you may be able to have a good guess), or if it was done with a brush
- whether extensions to letters were added with a different sized or shaped pen
- what was used as a writing fluid – bottled ink, diluted paint, Chinese stick-ink, etc.

All these factors control the shape of letters.

Though letters drawn by experts may look simple and quickly written (and some strokes may have been speedily produced), their serifs have often been built up with more than one pen stroke and constructed carefully with pen twists.

The letters used for the following writing are quite complex.

Normal Italic

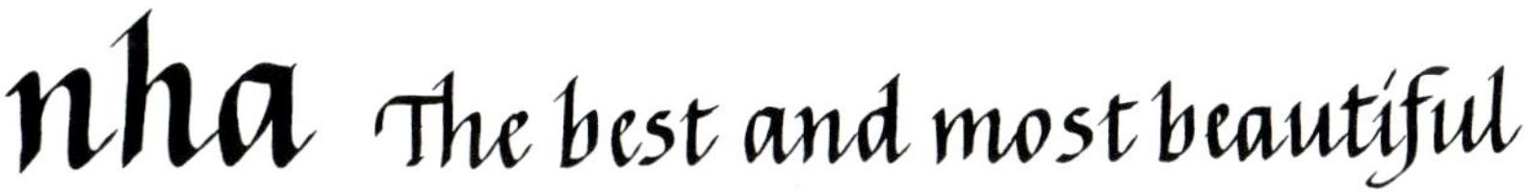

Addition of blocks (not traditional features) on some strokes and the pen lifted to create overlaps

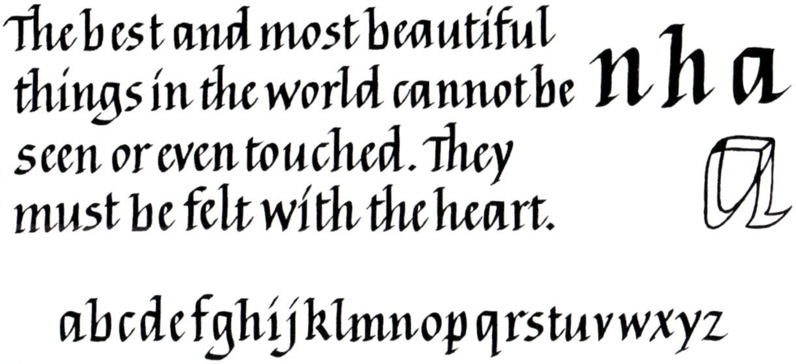

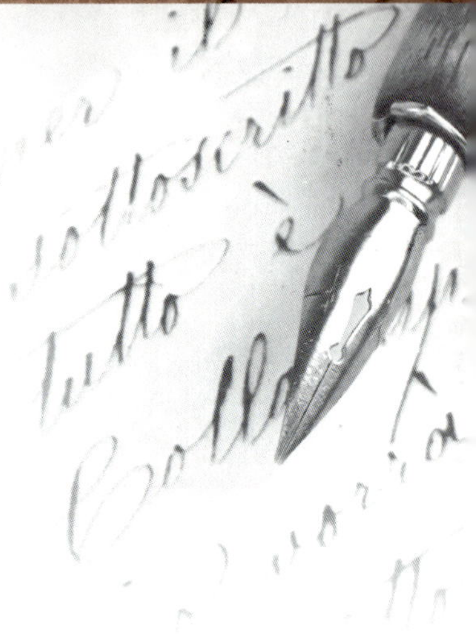

Using Your Calligraphy

CALLIGRAPHY CAN BE used traditionally for practical formal documents, such as certificates and invitations, and for poems and texts. Calligraphers also enjoy using letters for producing works of art on paper, sculptures, fabrics and a wide variety of other materials. No matter what will result from calligraphic activity, the aim is to produce work that is pleasing to the eye.

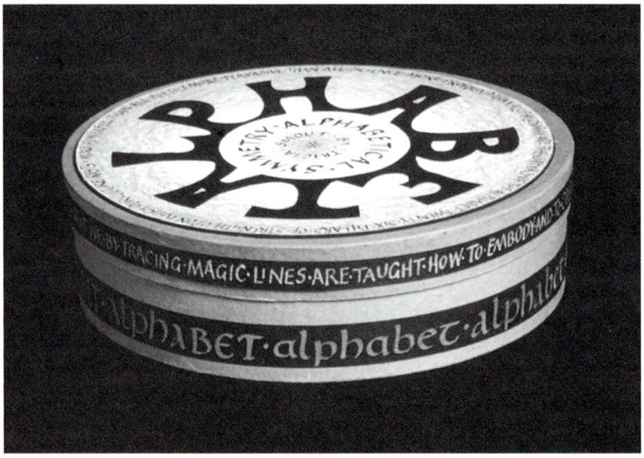

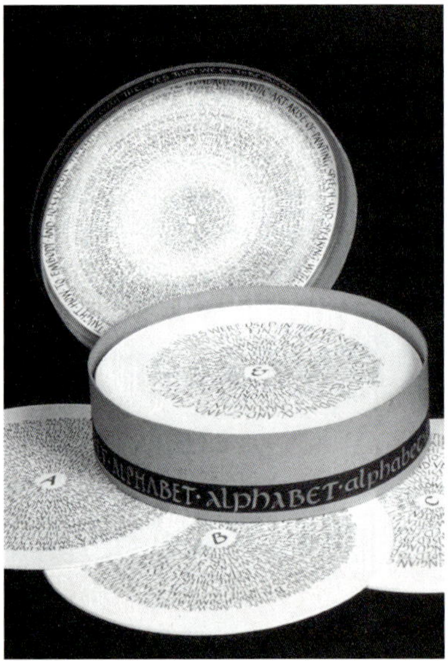

'Alphabet Box' by calligrapher and book artist Tricia Smout

When a calligrapher chooses to write something artistically, they will consider all possibilities for the layout, design and materials that are most appropriate to the text, their personal skills and the ways that they most enjoy working. Tricia Smout created this circular 'artist's book' (she has named her artist's book, 'Alphabet Box') as a set of circular boards that provide the historical development of each letter of the alphabet. On another occasion, a client may explain that they want to fit the finished piece in a picture frame to sit on a bedside table, or receive it as a folding book.

Laying out a page

The design and **layout** of a page or piece of calligraphic artwork is as personal as a painted picture, but calligraphy written on a single sheet, or a page of a book, always looks more impressive if you leave generous margins. It's hard to plan the size and spacing of lettering when you are given a sheet of paper and asked to fit a text into a particular area. Neither beginners nor professionals enjoy working this way. It's much easier to write on a larger piece of paper and trim the margins later to what you think looks nicest (probably equal-sized borders on the top and sides, and about 1½ times that size on the bottom).

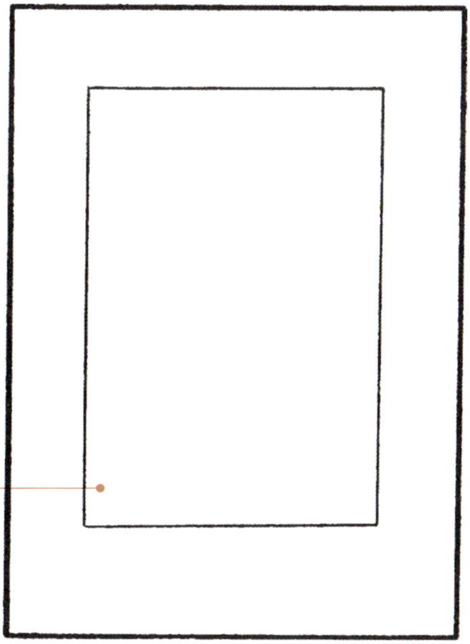

The inner box shows the area where it is aimed to fit the writing so that elegant margins will be provided.

When the pages of a book are planned, the margins closest to the spine will be reduced. Again, their size will largely be a matter of taste, but you could consider making each of the centre margins a fraction wider than half the width of the edge margins. This will give three equal white stripes – the extra fraction compensating for the curve of the paper in the middle or the sewing thread showing. You always write the pages before sewing them together.

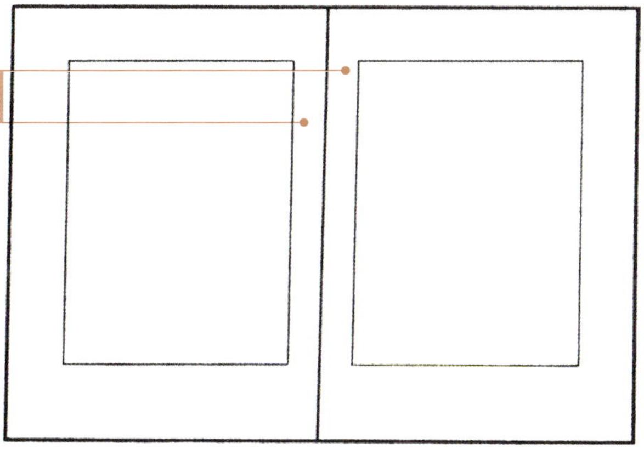

Margins closest to the spine have been reduced.

Titles and headings

Many calligraphers, in particular beginner calligraphers, usually find it much easier to write titles and headings in a mixture of capitals (majuscules) and small letters (minuscules), rather than all in capitals. To make the title stand out, make the size of the letters larger than those used for the text, and bolder (heavier weight).

This means that if the text letters are written 5 nib-widths high, you might use a wider nib and construct the letters of the title not only taller, but also only 4 or 4½ nib-widths high. The title and the author's and calligrapher's names are always the last thing I add to a poem. Here are some traditional layouts:

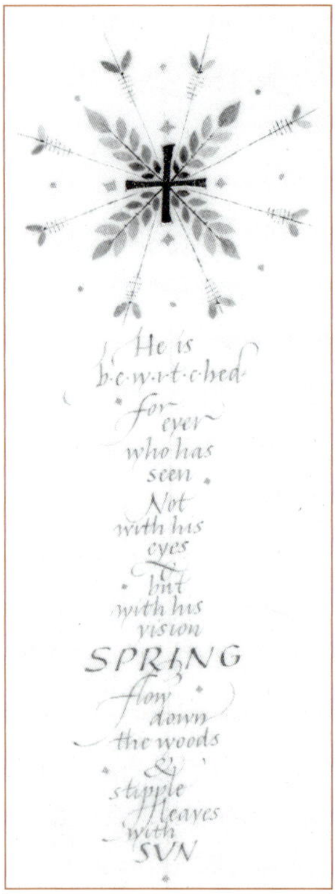

An example of centred text. From the collection of Barbara Nichol, The Pen Shoppe, Brisbane, calligraphy by Ann Hechle

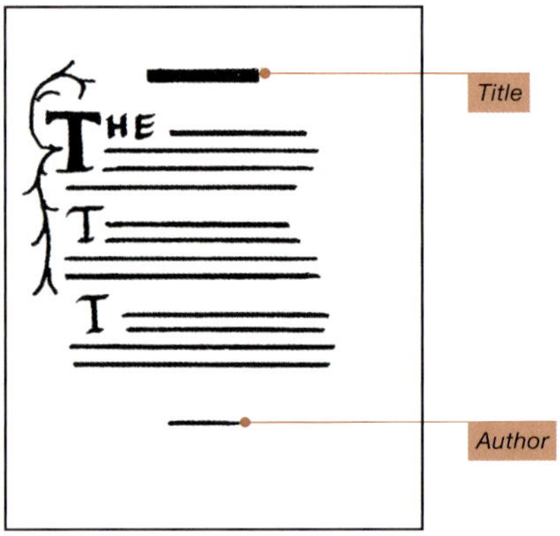

Aligned left

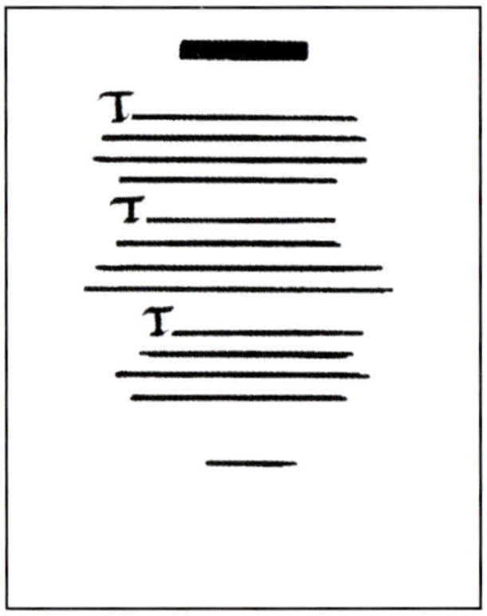

Centred

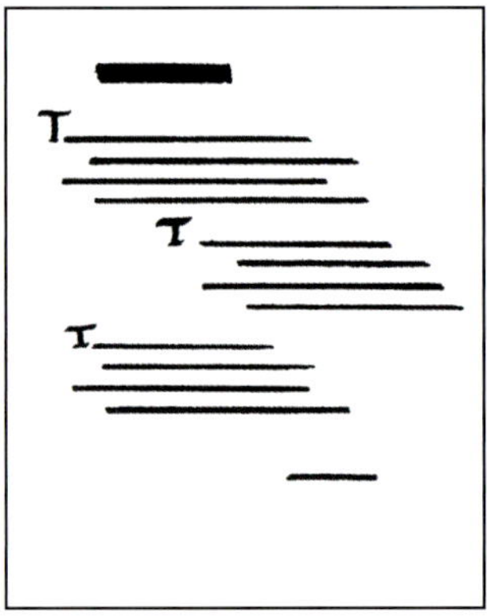

Alternated start of verses

Add:
Text first
Author second
Title last, to give visual balance

To find the best place to fit the title and the credits, I write them out on separate pieces of scrap paper and then shuffle these around until everything looks like it's in the right place. I can then draw guidelines there, and by holding my scrap-paper copies underneath, know where to start and finish writing.

Centred text and adding names

The scrap-paper technique can be used for producing documents, invitations, poems, sayings and anything that needs to be centred on a sheet of paper or card, or to write a name in a space. The text is carefully written with correct spacing on scrap paper, measured to find the middle of the writing and a mark is added there. This copy is folded so that the letters of the well-written rough copy can be held close to the guideline so that you can see what and where to write, and then the final version is added.

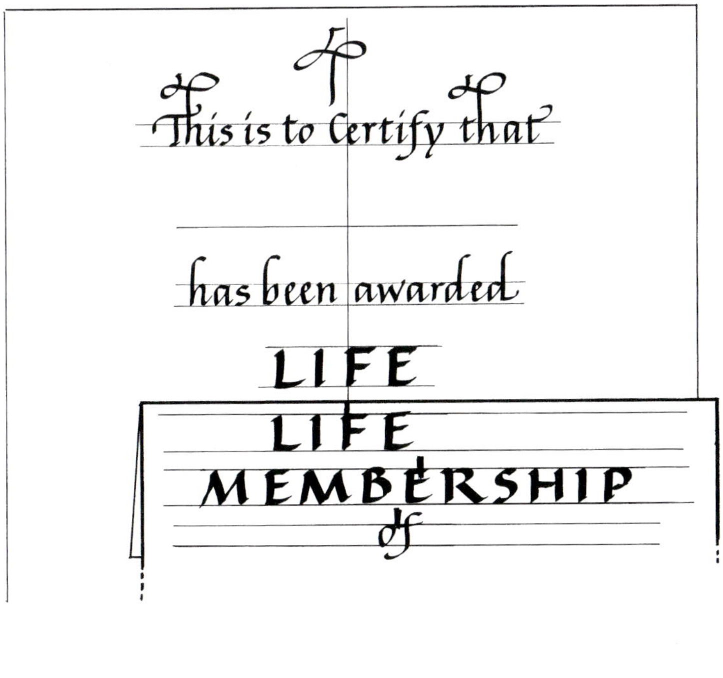

Follow the steps below to create a master copy of an invitation that will have folds running between lines of writing.

1. Write on a proportionally larger-sized piece of paper so that the writing can later be reduced to fit the space.
2. Multiply all measurements on the actual invitation by an equal amount and, using this proportional figure, mark the positions of the corners and fold lines on your writing sheet.
3. Plan where the lines of writing will go. Try to arrange for the writing to go either side of where the folds will be. Whatever you have chosen for the normal spacing between lines, increase this by at least half as much again where the folds will go.
4. Leave enough space for guest names to be written larger than most of the printed words.
5. If lettering is to be done in more than one size, make the difference obvious by choosing pens that differ significantly in width.

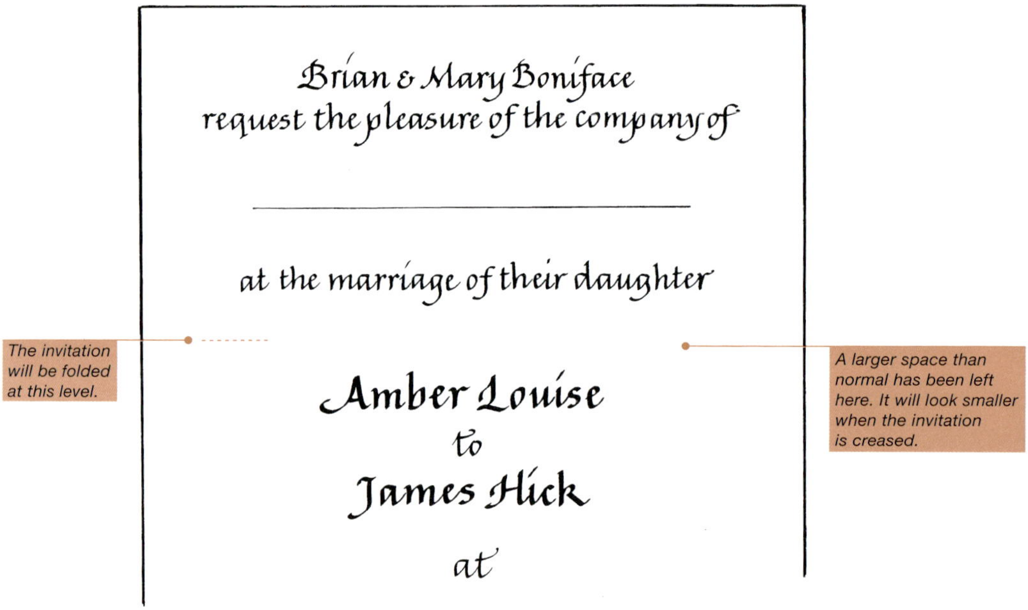

Do all writing in black ink, ready for the printer to photograph. The printer can blend ink to make copies in whatever colour you wish.

When it's time to set up the invitations on a press, the printer will photo-reduce your master copy so that the words fit perfectly.

When filling names into spaces on invitations, place cards and certificates, you probably don't need to measure the centre of each – you can just shuffle your rough copy around to judge the name's right place and then write over the top. But here's a tip, particularly if you have spare copies: if there are two words to be added, fill in the second one first. If the right-hand end of this word doesn't end up in quite the expected place, you can balance that by where you then start the first word of the name. You will always get the whole thing in the centre that way, but the space between the two words may be slightly wider or narrower than you originally intended.

The same sort of thing can be done when adding Mr & Mrs 'X', or any words separated by 'and'. Preferably, use an **ampersand**, and write everything to the right of it first, then balance the end point and the beginning point, and add the ampersand last. If a larger gap than expected is left, you can give the ampersand a stretch, or, particularly if you use the following shape (which I do for Italic), you can make it look elegant and natural by compressing it into a smaller gap.

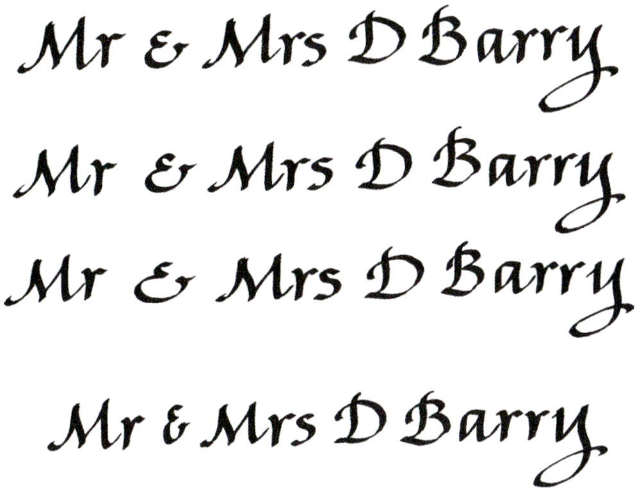

Normal spacing

Large space

Very large space

Small space

I prefer to write on place cards without a printed guideline – especially when both the first and family name have to be added. I write the names, staggered and close to each other on ordinary lined writing paper, trying to make sure any flourishes don't collide with other letters. When I write the finished card, I again write the second name first, then balance it with the first name.

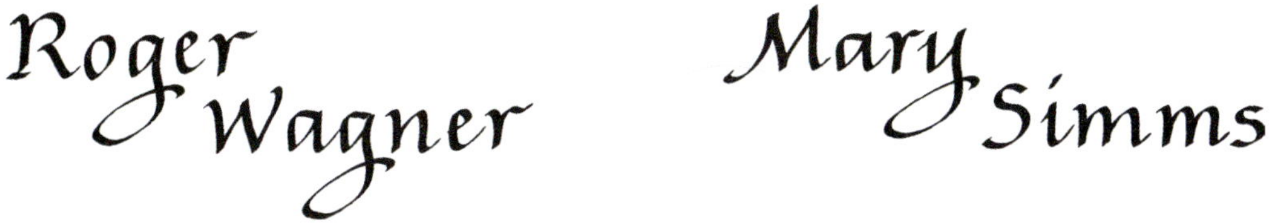

More designs

It's always difficult to write words around a circle or tight curve and have the letters look evenly spaced. You may have to alter the size of some exit strokes. Experts with much experience may try to modify letter shapes, but most people will find it easiest to write letters with parallel strokes (like 'm's and 'n's) normally but with their mid-points lined up with a radius, as shown.

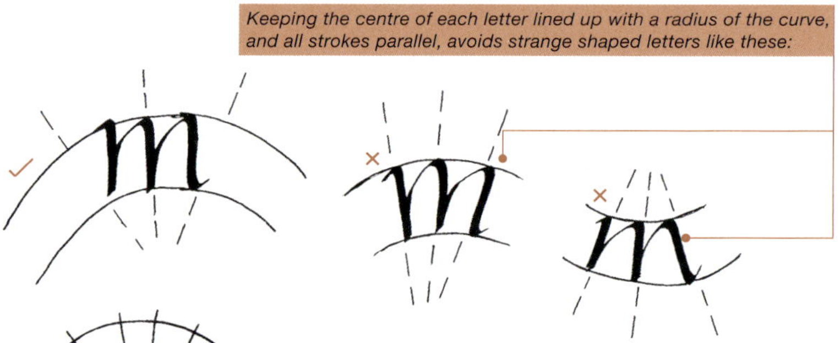

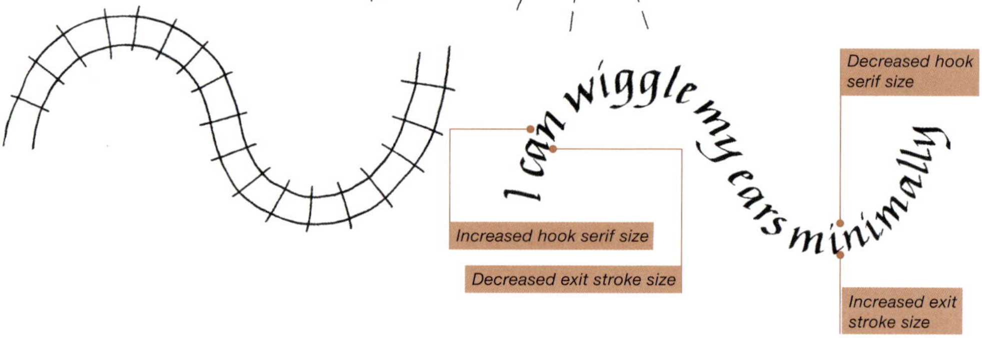

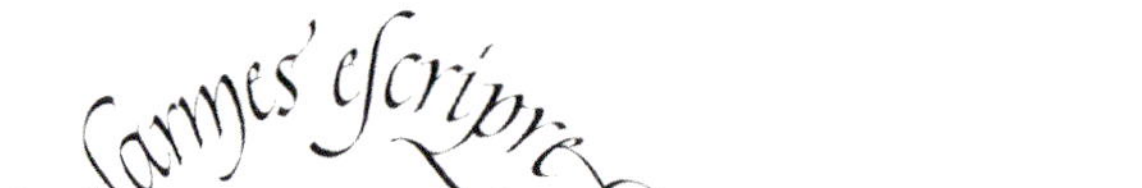

Calligraphy by Vincent Geneslay

In a single piece of calligraphy, you can mix more than one writing style, even for formal documents. **Running Book Hand** capitals, for example, are always a good accompaniment to Italic, and Italic and Uncial letters close to each other can be effective, too. Changing the writing style and weight or boldness of letters is an artistic way in which calligraphers express themselves or the ideas in the text they are writing. Let your imagination guide you.

'Dear Pig, are you willing
to sell for one shilling
your ring?'

A heavy weight Italic-based script with block additions

Said the Piggy,

Light weight traditional Italic

'I will.'

Half-Uncial

SO·THEY·TOOK·IT·AWAY
AND·WERE·MARRIED·NEXT·DAY
BY·THE·TURKEY·WHO·LIVES·ON·THE·HILL

Running Book Hand Roman Capitals

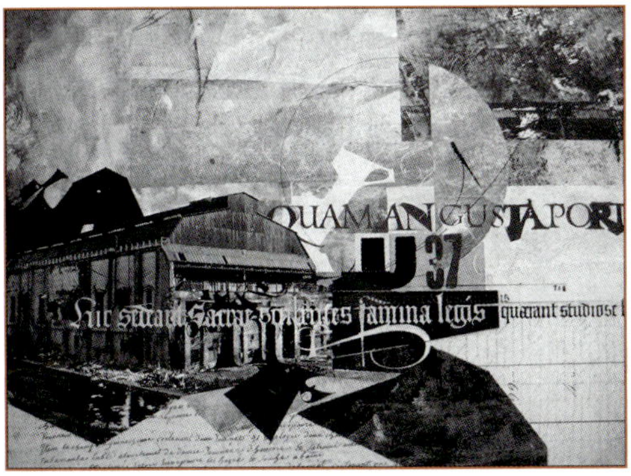

This is a very interesting mix of ancient and modern letters in several styles. Calligraphy by Laurant Pflughaupt

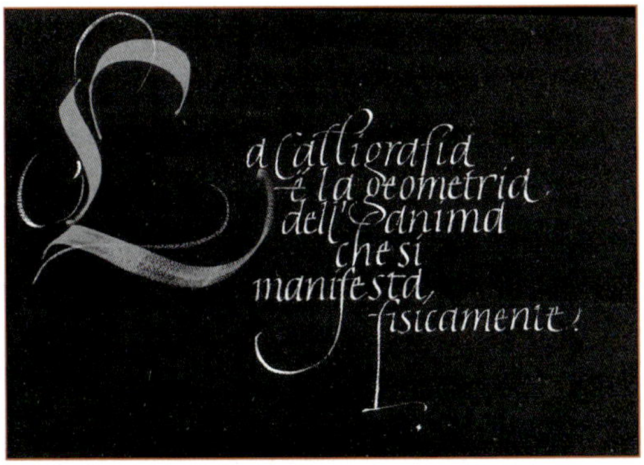

Super Italic with an interesting contrast in the capital. Calligraphy by Massimo Polello

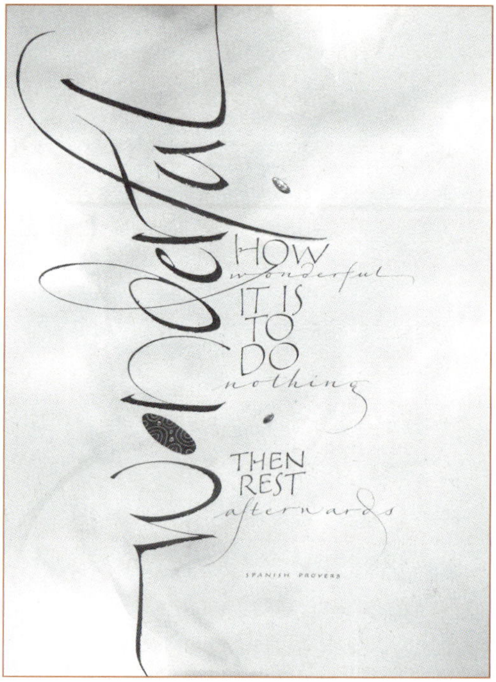

This piece of calligraphy shows a mixing of styles and pens.
Calligraphy by Julie Williams

A good way to plan complex designs is to draw many different thumb-nail pictures showing possible contrasts in weight and size of letters, and the positions of words.

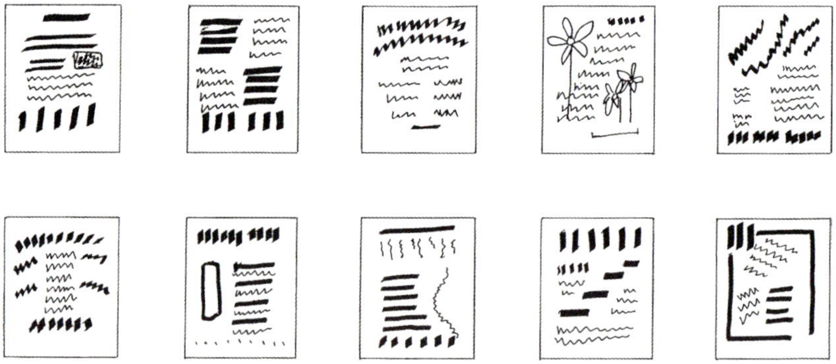

After you make a choice, the words can be written out on scrap paper, possibly several times, to determine exactly which writing style and size of **script** and line spacing will look best, and how long each line of text will be when it's finished. All parts of the final design can be cut out from rough sheets and assembled on another sheet of paper for a final visual check and to allow preparation to be made for the final copy.

Glossary

Alfred Fairbank	Alfred Fairbank, an English calligrapher, was born in 1895 and died in 1982. He wrote several books on calligraphy including *A Handwriting Manual*. He developed 'Italic' with joins as an elegant handwriting style and promoted it being taught in schools.
ampersand	A symbol sometimes used instead of the word 'and' (&).
ascenders	The sections of letters that rise above the top level of small letters, for example the top parts of 'l' or 'h'.
baseline	The normal bottom writing line on which letters sit.
black-letter calligraphy	Narrow letters with angular tops in dense Gothic letter styles.
book of Kells	The book of Kells is a beautifully handwritten Irish manuscript which dates back to the 7th century. It was written by monks on calf-skin vellum and is famous for its ornate decoration. The manuscript has been housed at Trinity College in Dublin since the mid 19th century.
bowl	The rounded part of a letter that encloses space – for example, in a 'b' or 'p'.
Carolingian style	The features of Carolingian style include a slight forward lean, wide rounded letters, blobby tops and bouncy writing rhythm.
compress	To draw letters narrower than usual.
copybooks	Books consisting of Calligraphy that can be copied for practice.
counter	The space that your eyes tell you is enclosed in a letter.
descenders	The tails of letters like 'g' and 'p' that hang down below the level of the bottom of normal small letters.
Donald Jackson	Donald Jackson is a famous English calligrapher. He was born in Lancashire, England in 1938. When he was 13 years old, he won he won a scholarship to art school. As a teenager his first ambition was to be 'The Queen's Scribe' and his second ambition was to inscribe and illuminate the Bible. He has achieved both of these.
Edward Johnston	Edward Johnston was an English calligraphy who lived from 1872 to 1944. He designed the script known as Foundational Hand.
flourishes	Flamboyant endings to pen strokes or letter parts, often with loops or exaggerated features.
gouache	Artist's quality opaque poster print.
hackle	Decorative and sometimes lengthened comma – shaped additions to a letter.

hairline	The thinnest line or mark that a pen nib can make.
Irene Wellington	Irene Wellington was a famous English calligrapher who lived from 1904–1984. She was a founder of modern calligrapher. She used letters and layouts to express personal feelings.
layout	A plan of what goes where on a page to create the finished design.
Lindisfarne Gospels	The Lindisfarne Gospels were written and intricately illuminated around the 8th century. They were once held at the British Museum but, since 1973, they have been housed at the British Library in London.
nib	The writing point of a pen.
nib-widths	Also known as pen-widths. Used to determine the height of letters.
pen angle	The angle between the straight edge of the pen nib, or the finest line that it is made by sliding it, and a horizontal writing line.
Queen's scribe	The Queen's scribe is responsible for using perfect lettering to prepare the most important state documents and then illuminating them with gold. The Queen's scribe is also known as the Scribe to the Crown Office of Her Majesty Queen Elizabeth the Second. Donald Jackson has been the Queen's scribe since 1964.
quill	A swan's, goose's or other big bird's wing feather that has been treated, prepared and cut to make a pen.
Ramsey Psalter	A 10th century book of psalms, which could have been written in Ramsey or Winchester, in England, and intended for abbey use or private use by the abbey's founder, Oswald. The script was studied by Edward Johnston and used as a model for the development of his Foundational Hand.
Running Book Hand	A modern version of Carolingian.
script	Writing styles; letter shapes with family resemblances.
serif	Additions to the starting and finishing points on letter strokes – for example, hooks, slabs and wedges.
skeleton letters	The simplest possible shapes of letters, made up only of thin line drawings.
slabs	A horizontal brick-shaped serif or addition to a letter stroke, but it could be thin or have sloping ends. A slab sticks out on both sides of the stroke, but a half-slab only protrudes from one side.
weight	The relationship between the width of the pen nib used and the height of letters drawn. A letter of a fixed height has a heavier weight when written with a wider nib.
x-height	The height of normal small letters, like 'a' and 'e', without ascenders and descenders. Also known as 'body-height'.